Brothers & Beasts

Brothers & Beasts

AN ANTHOLOGY OF MEN ON FAIRY TALES

Edited by Kate Bernheimer

WITH A FOREWORD BY MARIA TATAR AND AN AFTERWORD BY JACK ZIPES

WAYNE STATE UNIVERSITY PRESS DETROIT

Manufactured in the United States of America.

11 10 09 08 07   5 4 3 2 1

Library of Congress Cataloging-in-Publication Data

Brothers and beasts : an anthology of men on fairy tales / edited by
Kate Bernheimer ; with a foreword by Maria Tatar and an afterword
by Jack Zipes.
        p. cm. — (Series in fairy-tale studies)
    ISBN-13: 978-0-8143-3267-2 (pbk. : alk. paper)
    ISBN-10: 0-8143-3267-6 (pbk. : alk. paper)
1. American literature—Male authors—History and criticism—
Theory, etc.   2. Men and literature—United States—History—20th
century.   3. Authors, American—20th century—Books and reading.
4. Fairy tales—United States—History and criticism.   5. Fairy tales
in literature.   6. Folklore in literature.   7. Authorship.
I. Bernheimer, Kate.   II. Bernheimer, Kate.
    PS153.M33B76 2007
    810.9'9287
                                                        2007017898

⊖ The paper used in this publication meets the minimum require-
ments of the American National Standard for Information
Sciences—Permanence of Paper for Printed Library Materials,
ANSI Z39.48-1984.

Erik Kraft's "I Consider My Luck" first appeared in *Passionate Spectator,*
New York: St. Martin's Press, 2004. © Erik Kraft 2004. Reprinted by
permission of the author and publisher.

Neil Gaiman's poems first appeared in the following publications:
"Instructions": *A Wolf at the Door and Other Retold Fairy Tales,* ed. Ellen
Datlow and Terri Windling. New York: Simon & Schuster Books
for Young Readers, 2000. © Neil Gaiman 2000.

"Inventing Aladdin": *Swan Sisters: Fairy Tales Retold,* ed. Ellen
Datlow and Terri Windling. New York: Simon & Schuster Books
for Young Readers, 2003. © Neil Gaiman 2003.

"Boys and Girls Together": *Black Heart, Ivory Bones,* ed. Ellen
Datlow and Terri Windling. New York: Avon Books, 2000.
© Neil Gaiman 2000.

"Locks": *Silver Birch, Blood Moon,* ed. Ellen Datlow and Terri Windling.
New York: Avon Books, 1999. © Neil Gaiman 1999.

Designed by Isaac Tobin
Typeset by The Composing Room of Michigan, Inc
Composed in Clifford Six and Clifford Nine
Cover and interior art by Lauren Nassef

FOR ANDY, FOR BRENT, AND FOR MY FATHER

In full confidence that you, my dear sir, will be persuaded by the usefulness and urgency of our cause which with the day-to-day ever more increasing devastating decline and disappearance of our folk customs can no longer be postponed without great harm, we hope you will offer our undertaking a helping hand and . . . for this reason you have been selected as a member of this society. The society wishes to collect data with silent diligence and . . . each person does whatever he can, whenever he can, where and how he chooses.

JACOB GRIMM, *Short Circular*, 1815
(excerpted from a translation by Alan Dundes)

CONTENTS

"For a long time I scorned fairy tales," Norman Lock tells us
with faintly Proustian regret. With their wishful thinking and
imaginative flourishes, fairy tales have become tarnished by
their escapist excesses and, all too rapidly, they cease to work
their magic as we grow up.

Fairy-tale scholars often note that the fairy tale called "Hansel
and Gretel" belongs mainly to Gretel. After all, Gretel's the one
who outwits the witch with that bone. From the little book of
the tale that I had as a child, I remember Hansel always depicted in fear. On one page he trembled in the margin, lost;
later, locked with his sister inside a room, he cowered in a corner, near where I'd dog-eared the book. This page also was torn
halfway down its middle; I had once tried to rip it out.

"All good fairy tales have meaning on many levels," Bruno Bet-
tleheim observes in *The Uses of Enchantment*. "Only the child can

know which meanings are of significance to him at the moment."

Wild forests of broken brambles and damp moss and pines moaning like women in labor or cows.

Most of this story is made of coincidences. Moments that could or could not mean what they could mean. For example, on a winter afternoon my boyfriend looks up from what he is reading as I am about to run an errand with the car. I am at a cabin in the New Hampshire woods, where I've gone to do some writing, and he is visiting. I have the keys in my hand.

Tale is the underbelly of myth. Myth is head, tale body; myth power, tale resistance; myth nice, tale naughty; myth structure, tale flow; myth king, tale fool; myth sacred, tale profane; myth father, tale child (though the child, as always, is the father's father); myth tragic, tale comic.

I don't honestly know what I think about fairy tales, because they are part of me. It would be like trying to explain what I think of my spine or my circulatory system or my eyes. The tales I read as a boy define how I see the world and how I perceive what I see; they flow through me, and, sometimes still, they hold me up.

I grew up in Skåne, the southernmost province of Sweden, consisting mainly of farmland. In many of the fields there are burial mounds from the Bronze Age (ten to fifteen feet tall). My grade-school class used to go to play at one of these mounds in a field just outside Håstad, the small town where the school was located. This particular mound was unusual: there was a large gash in the side of it.

A slender girl and her mother lived in our town, good people but poor. They had nothing to eat, like everyone else in our town. The girl was always wandering in the forest. She walked, snapping the branches, scaring the squirrels, looking for something to put in her mouth. Here the page turns.

I used to think that "Jack and the Beanstalk" was about luck, and dumb luck at that. As I remembered the tale, Jack was a dull boy, a sluggard, who complained when his mother sent him to town to sell the cow, their only remaining asset, so that they could buy some food. Whenever Jack came to mind, as he has from time to time over the years, I saw him trudging along a dusty country road, reluctantly, tugging the cow along behind him.

For a long time I scorned fairy tales, parables, and fables as children's or folk literature, as a less-evolved narrative form. I was taught this attitude. If not instructed in it, at least I came away from college with this prejudice. Who knows who or what put it there more than thirty years ago? But eventually, in my forties, I came to appreciate them.

Thank you for bearing with me through all this, and may your *ever afters* all qualify as happy ones. In conclusion, dear readers, let me just state again that structure turned on its head is still structure. Or, said another way, structure still is, head its on turned, structure. Forth-to-back and back-to-forth equally rely on the strong preposition "to," the preposition of intention. What have you been reading about for the past twenty minutes but precisely this? What am I writing about now? A silly game and I apologize, dear readers—or dearly taxed and sorely vexed readers.

German Catholic boy from St. Paul. The boy and the girl got married and lived happily ever after in the city (and, later, the suburbs) with their four children. I don't remember it, but I know that my dad used to read me stories of Robin Hood and King Arthur, much as his older brother had done for him.

My first exposure, or the first exposure I can remember, to the pleasures of narrative happened when I was a little over two years old, in Bangalore, in the second half of the 1950s.

Why make a map? Why do anything at all? Not how, because hows are easy, series or sequence, one foot after the other, but existentially why bother, what does it solve? Well, if you don't need to, don't. Wouldn't that be great? Just don't make anything.

The suspect was "not your average maggot-looking dope dealer on the corner." At least that's what the police say. It was 1994, and he was arrested for possession of bufotenine, a Schedule 1 drug under the California Controlled Substances Act. The drug in question came in the form of four toads—Hanz, Franz, Peter, and Brian—that the suspect intended to smoke. Not the entire toad, but, as has been known to happen in fairy tales, its skin.

The first bear may be uncouth, but not unkind, despite appearances. His English isn't good and he lives alone in a cottage in the forest, but no one can say he doesn't try. If he didn't try, if the idea of trying, and thus of restraint, were alien to him, the first bear wouldn't live in a cottage at all. He'd live in the deep forest and all anyone would see of him, before the end, would be hard eyes and the dark barrel of his muzzle.

My grandparents lived within a mile of the ocean, and in the summer I'd stay with them. In the mornings my grandmother and I would walk down to the beach, to the edge of the water, and she'd lay down a towel and sit there for hours and watch me swim. When I'd take a break she'd give me money and I'd run up to the food stand they had there, and I'd order us lunch and bring it back to her. She was a great old lady.

There is something putatively magical about an afterword. The term suggests that there is more worth saying than what has already been written, as if the afterword can provide a magic touch with a happy ending to a book that needs resolution.

Maria Tatar

FOREWORD

"For a long time I scorned fairy tales," Norman Lock tells us with faintly Proustian regret. With their wishful thinking and imaginative flourishes, fairy tales have become tarnished by their escapist excesses and, all too rapidly, they cease to work their magic as we grow up. Girls may be allowed to indulge their desires to read about multi-towered castles surrounded by rose hedges and about princesses who dance nightly in enchanted realms, but boys are far less likely to remain absorbed into adolescence by stories framed in our culture as satisfying feminine desires. "Boys might surrender to the pleasures fairy tales offered before they were taught otherwise," Marina Warner writes, "but they soon sternly put them away like skipping and doll's houses, and would scoff from their superior world of electric trains and airforce yarns."

For many of the authors represented in this collection, the prodigies and wonders of fairy tales became, at an early age, forbidden pleasures, and they were often obediently set aside for the intellectual challenges of "adult" literature. And yet stories about singing bones, giants living in beanstalks, siblings abandoned in the woods, girls who spew diamonds or toads, and cats sporting boots were—as these essays make clear—never really banished from the imagination but remained powerful navigational instruments, charting paths through real-life experience and helping to find ways to cope with it. Fantasy worlds, as Wallace Stevens reminds us, help us to visualize actual worlds, building sturdy bridges to fears and desires that we encounter on a daily basis. And they also promise utopian possibilities: "It never happened in real life," Steve Almond writes, "but it did happen every time I read *Mrs. Piggle-Wiggle*."

The Brothers and Beasts who contributed to this volume found in fairy tales a way to escape reality, but they also read the stories to escape into opportunities. In a poignant memoir about childhood reading, Francis Spufford stressed how stories stage possibilities, creating a theater of what could be, might be, or should be: "I wanted to pass through a portal, and by doing so to pass from rusty reality with its scaffolding of facts and events into the freedom of story. I wanted doors. If, in a story, you found the one panel that was hinged, and it opened, and it turned out that behind the walls flashed the gold and peacock blue of something else . . . all possibilities would be renewed." It was Aristotle who observed that the poet's function is not to describe "the thing that has happened, but a kind of thing that might happen." Stories allow us to think in a subjunctive or utopian mood, keeping us anchored in reality yet also opening up what Brian Baldi describes, in this volume, as "a new space where readers can be limber, hazard their own routes, and make new associations and extrapolations about life."

And yet, what happens when the story ends? Or when the pleasures of storytelling are banished in favor of the reality principle? The writers of these essays reveal that child readers carry into their adult lives imagined transitional objects charged with the same power as D. W. Winnicott's teddy bears and blankets to comfort, reassure, and serve as a defense against anxieties. These invented objects often distill the essence of a story. They are the props to which Timothy Schaffert refers, the whimsical, magical, and haunting paraphernalia of the fairy-tale world: "a poisoned apple with one toothy bite missing, a spinning wheel, a radish stolen from a garden, a glass slipper, a glass coffin, a windowpane of sugar, a spindle, a shuttle, a needle." Far more important than the melodramatic twists and turns of fairy-tale plots, these props often serve as the inspiration for improvisations and new plots.

C. S. Lewis once famously remarked that, as a writer, he never developed a blueprint or narrative map for his children's novels: "Everything began with images: a faun carrying an umbrella, a queen on a sledge, a magnificent lion." The fabulous figures and objects embedded in fairy-tale narratives sometimes take on a life of their own, inspiring pleasure, curiosity, and desire. Who has not, as a child, dwelt with longing on the fabulous Turkish Delight given to Edmund in *The Lion, the Witch and the Wardrobe*? Lewis was himself drawn to the fairy tale as a genre because of "its brevity, its severe restraint on description, its flexible traditionalism, its inflexible hostility to all analysis, digression, reflections and 'gas.'" He instinctively recognized the attractions of surface beauty and the appeal to the child of objects that have the capacity to unlock imaginative possibilities, to let the mind wander even after the tale in which the objects appear has ended.

And yet, as the Brothers and Beasts remind us, fairy tales offer more than miniaturized fancy and compelling beauty. Jeff Vander-Meer is right to emphasize "the ferocity and animal intensity at the core of the past century's excesses" and how fairy tales manage to capture our collective fears. Wonder tales can transfix us with horror as well as with beauty, but they always also engage our intellectual powers, provoking forms of curiosity that lead us to explore what they describe and to understand that the beast lurking in the woods may be our next of kin. Like the women writers in the companion volume to this one, the men here are committed to more than moments of rapture. They relentlessly explore the dark side of fantasy, recognizing that violence and horror coexist with wonder and beauty.

In an essay on childhood reading Graham Greene reflected on its vertiginous effects, asking where we ever get anything these days to equal the "excitement and revelation" of those early years. When you read a book as a child, it sends chills up your spine and produces somatic effects that rarely accompany the reading experience of adults. Fairy tales can offer up a chamber of horrors— Bluebeard's dead wives, a witch shoved into an oven, a grandmother devoured by a wolf—and thereby create the desire to *keep reading*, to make sure that Fatima, Hansel, or Little Red Riding Hood will survive, and also to learn more about the great existential mysteries evoked in their stories.

In the very same decade that Graham Greene was reminiscing about his childhood reading, Richard Wright recalled—in an autobiographical account of growing up in the Jim Crow South—his first brush with fairy tales. Ella, a schoolteacher boarding at his house, read to him a story called "Bluebeard and His Seven Wives." "Once upon a time there was an old, old man named Bluebeard," she began in a low voice. And as she read, the young boy became so absorbed in the story that "the look of things" altered and a new reality replaced the sunlit porch on which they were reading. "Enchanted and enthralled," he lived in a world inhabited by "magical presences."

Ella never made it to the end of the story, for Wright's grandmother interrupted the reading, calling the fairy tale "devil's work." And, in a sense, given its associations with duplicity, transgression, and knowledge, it was. For that very reason, the reading experience became transformative for Wright: "I burned to learn to read novels and I tortured my mother into telling me the meaning of every strange word I saw, not because the word itself had any value, but because it was the gateway to a forbidden and enchanting land." Here excitement leads to revelation, to a transformative experience that recognizes the degree to which language—"strange words"—is the portal to knowledge and to an understanding of what really matters to us.

As children, boys and girls alike, we were all seduced by the attractions of magical thinking, in part because we lived in a state that the French philosopher François Lyotard has described as "being affected and not having the means, the language, the representation, to name, identify, reproduce and recognize what is affecting us." The excitement of fairy tales fuels the desire to understand all the "strange words" that constitute stories—words that have a magic power of their own in producing marvels and prodigies that have the power to change us.

Kate Bernheimer

Fairy-tale scholars often note that the fairy tale called "Hansel and Gretel" belongs mainly to Gretel. After all, Gretel's the one who outwits the witch with that bone.

From the little book of the tale that I had as a child, I remember Hansel always depicted in fear. On one page he trembled in the margin, lost; later, locked with his sister inside a room, he cowered in a corner, near where I'd dog-eared the book. This page also was torn halfway down its middle; I had once tried to rip it out. Though I wish I could say I'd done it to free them, I was not so bold. The picture frightened me, and I had wanted it gone. I was ambivalent about it, however, and finally had left it in—even marked it as a favorite, apparently, with that dog-ear.

In another picture, which scared me even more than those of the children almost being eaten, Gretel holds a chicken bone through bars, toward the witch's thin and ugly hand. This page was supposed to provide comfort to readers, I think, showing how the witch would be outwitted. Yet that chicken bone was somehow too horrible and I always averted my eyes.

I had a brother who was, much to my disappointment, not named Hansel, yet I was devoted to him. Our bedroom windows were kitty-corner to each other's, and on summer nights we would crank open the windows and whisper secrets from window to window about our sisters, both of whom were louder than we were. Because our rooms looked out on the woods—a suburban spread of oaks, maples, and pines—these secrets seemed even more magical to me. In summer, the scent of skunk cabbage wafted up at us and lent a thick perfume to the scene.

Despite all the scholarship I've read that so convincingly highlights Gretel's impressive agency in this particular Grimm Brothers tale, I don't remember adoring Gretel at all. In fact, I remember disliking her more than that witch—but why? Complicating matters for me, the name Gretel was shared by our family dog, a dachshund. How I loved Gretel the dog, yet how I feared Gretel the sister. Truly, I don't remember any fondness for her. Perhaps it was her very defiance that frightened me; I identified with the underdog in any tale, so it was my fervor for Hansel that made me love this tale, not my admiration of Gretel.

Perhaps because I was timid and shy, I identified with Hansel, who didn't do much except follow. Or perhaps I associated him with my younger brother, who had put up with so much from our sisters—such as their dressing him in a doll's gown and strolling him around town in a carriage.

And perhaps Gretel (the girl) seemed to me—in her defiance of the witch—a lot like our own older sister, whose agency controlled all of us, including the neighborhood woods we tromped through to gather tadpoles and flowers—she controlled everything in the universe, it seemed. And not only material things—the TV remote, potato chips, hand-me-downs—but also abstract things, such as who my parents loved most. Often she told us we were unwanted, because we were meek. (She has apologized profusely for such wanton cruelty back then—but in some ways I am grateful, for it taught me to despise bullies, a valuable lesson indeed.)

So it was that I loved Hansel and feared Gretel. And so it was that, as a young child, it escaped me that both Hansel *and* Gretel had been abandoned into that fearsome scene. My sense of the story was associative and irrational, a reading habit I have not entirely outgrown.

It was in this way that my idea of brothers began—that brothers were sweet and needed much saving.

So it was in another of my favorite tales, called "The Queen Bee." It is the story of the Most Brotherly Brother of All.

"The Queen Bee" begins with this promising line: "Two king's sons went in search of adventure, fell into a wild, dissolute way of life, and never came home again."

But "The Queen Bee" is not their story. It is the story of their youngest brother, known as Blockhead. He goes looking for the brothers who have gone in search of adventure. When he finds them, they scoff at him. They tease him relentlessly, in fact— mainly about his tenderness toward nature. "Leave them alone," Blockhead says of an anthill, some ducks, and a beehive, defending them against these wild brothers. How they ridicule him for his tenderness!

Eventually the brothers arrive at a castle, and there a little gray man gives the brothers the chance to release the castle from its long spell. I won't go into the details here, which are long, but suffice it to say that the two dissolute ones immediately fail and are turned to stone. Yet, though Blockhead has great desire to help the little gray man, this proves rather difficult for him. He is a Blockhead, after all, despite his great love of nature, of other things even more helpless than he.

Finally, hopelessly, he sits down on the earth and cries. And at that time, grateful for his protections, all of the animals rally upon his behalf, helping him find the lips of a girl who's eaten some honey. This, of course, releases the little gray man's spell, and the girl who's eaten the honey becomes Blockhead's wife. (The little gray man is not mentioned again in the story, but I'm certain that he rejoices.)

My brother shares a birthday, October 2, with one of our favorite fictional characters from childhood, good old Charlie Brown. Like a fairy-tale character, Charlie Brown lives in a land inhabited by many children, the parents very distant from the story indeed. *Peanuts* comics, like fairy tales, also reside in a truly existential plane; Linus was the first philosopher I ever encountered in print. Also, Charlie's friends—the dogs and the birds—can speak and have feelings; this too is like fairy tales, where all things are everything.

And Charlie Brown's nickname was Blockhead.

So this is how, for me, the story of the benevolent brother Block-head got mixed up with my own brother, with Charlie Brown. And this is an example of how a young child fell in love with fairy tales, with the rapture that came from forgetting what was real and what was imagined—what was a story and what had really happened. In fairy tales nothing was what it seemed. Things collapsed into things. Also, nothing turned out quite as you expected; in other words, the seemingly fragile turned strong, survived against all the odds. The meek shall inherit, and so on.

All this contributed to the beauty of fairy tales, and it was all bound up, always and fiercely, with my love for my brother, that quiet one.

As I got older, I became not so afraid of Gretel. Rather, I began to imagine Hansel and Gretel as twins, or more. One not-girl and one not-boy but rather entwined into one being, they were incapable of surviving alone. Not so much gendered as engendering each other. Brother and sister—a compound noun.

It is my deep love for fairy tales—truly an obsession of mine—that directed me to collect the essays contained in this book. Because I consider fairy tales a brilliant, shimmering art form, and because they are a bit of a literary underdog, I find myself driven to protect them. By reading fairy tales and by retelling them to ourselves and each other, we not only celebrate this stunning aesthetic form but also their potential to help us understand our existence in a world brimming with violence, nature, power, and loss. The fairy-tale tradition will continue as long as we revisit the stories, and the revisiting provides the potential to transform the old into new. Indeed, "what makes a fairy tale new," Jack Zipes has said, "is predicated on new insights in a complex world that baffles and frustrates us. Fairy tales provide us with the tools, aesthetic tools, to cope with a rapidly changing world." The simple premise that new insights into tales can help celebrate and preserve the tradition, along with my personal obsession with fairy tales, was the inspiration for this collection of essays.

Yet this book almost didn't happen at all. To explain, I consider this collection to be a companion to a book I gathered years ago called *Mirror, Mirror on the Wall: Women Writers Explore Their Favorite Fairy Tales*. When I began working on that book, it was called something else—*Into the Mirror: An Anthology of Writers on Fairy Tales*. From that title you might gather that I intended it to include essays by all sorts of writers—that is, essays by both women and men. Several people who greatly supported that book did not support the inclusion of men. They claimed, quite adamantly, "No one will be interested in what men have to say about fairy tales." Worse still, they continued, "Men wouldn't have much of interest to say about fairy tales."

But evidence of men's interest in fairy tales is vast and spans many centuries. At the time I was very young and did not argue. Besides, I thought that a book gathering essays by women would be interesting too. Why not? But I always considered that book incomplete—or, more precisely, because I am an emotional editor, I consider it unfair. Of all the literary traditions, the fairy-tale tradition is generous and spiteful toward both boys and girls, men and women—it does not prefer one over the other. I did not like to suggest that women, more than men, had a stake in these powerful stories.

Also, I felt that the assertion that men would have nothing to say about fairy tales was reflective of a twofold prejudice: against men and against fairy tales. There was an implied disdain for boys drawn to stories of wonder. There was also an implied disdain for fairy tales, so strongly associated with girls and the nursery.

Though several eloquent gender studies of fairy tales exist, one hardly encounters a popular reference to men and fairy tales—Robert Bly's *Iron John* notwithstanding. It is as if men are not allowed to have an emotional or artistic relationship to fairy tales. On the whole—in the classroom, at conferences, or at lectures—I find that men are not accustomed to being asked if they like fairy tales, let alone whether fairy tales have influenced their emotional, intellectual, and artistic lives.

The premise of this diverse collection is to reverse that poor spell. There is truly no agenda beyond that simple desire of wanting to discover what these men would say about fairy tales. I was willing to coax them along their way. Plain and simple, I hope, in a fairy-tale way: in fairy tales it is often the humble to whom magic is revealed.

So I wrote to authors whose work I felt owed something—whether overtly or mysteriously—to fairy tales. It was difficult to pare down the list, but I approached writers who work in a range of forms—poetry, essay, memoir, novel. I made no discrimination between those writers considered "literary" and those considered "popular," nor between those considered "experimental" or "mainstream." I feel that such categories have little to say to the fairy-tale tradition, a tradition so open and varied, as friendly to abstraction as to precision, as friendly to mice as to men.

I asked these writers, "Would you be interested in writing a personal essay about fairy tales for a collection?" That was the invitation. I wanted the invitation to be as open ended as a fairy tale that begins "Once upon a time . . ." and then goes somewhere surprising, unknown.

Interestingly, while for *Mirror, Mirror* I had too many commitments from writers very rapidly, with the men it was not so easy. It is not that they had nothing to say, they told me, but rather that they had *too much* to say. Invited contributors told me, by way of declining, that fairy tales were of tantamount importance to their work, and this was too large a topic to consider in the time allotted (please note that I was offering nearly two years). In fact, several writers said, no one else had noticed the intimate relationship to fairy tales in their work before and they couldn't believe that I had—how amazing, they thought they had kept it a secret. I'm not making this up—it happened repeatedly. That is the second reason this collection nearly did not happen. Yet even among those who claimed the subject too precious to attempt in an essay, many finally agreed—as I left the correspondence open, asking them just to "let me know" if they changed their mind.

Change—a movement so entwined with the tales. Change they did.

Nonetheless I received so many anguished correspondences in the process of gathering this book that I began to worry that I had asked something of these writers that was really causing them to suffer. "I can't write the essay after all," more than one told me in a painful phone call that would go something like this: "It is simply too personal an endeavor, I'm afraid. I'm awfully sorry." I would murmur in compassion, express my regret. (As an experienced editor, I know the difference between an excuse from a writer and the real thing, and these intimate correspondences were not excuses.)

Of course, as evidenced by this collection, you may gather that days or weeks later I would receive a gorgeous essay from that very same person—it would just suddenly appear on my desk without explanation.

What magical agent had intervened? I think simply the magic of fairy tales.

The initial fear, perhaps, had something to do with our cultural bias against boys' liking fairy tales. Also, for many writers, as Ursula Le Guin points out in *Mirror, Mirror,* fairy tales are the very definition of the anxiety of influence. Without presuming to psychoanalyze my generous contributors, I do think their anxiety about writing for *Brothers and Beasts* was increased because they were uneasy with writing about stories that the broader popular culture associates so deeply with girls. One high-profile prospective contributor declined for this reason, saying he'd mar his reputation with a "primarily male readership" if he wrote about fairy tales. That made me sad.

And in striking contrast to his depressing reason for not writing, those brave men who did contribute make me glad. Without regard for the commercial prospects of the book or their "manhood," they wrote.

This book is a testament to fairy tales and their living influence on art. It is not, however, a treatise on men and fairy tales, on the relationship of gender to fairy tales—though surely scholars will draw interesting conclusions from individual essays in the book. What this collection provides is the chance to hear stories about the intimate relationship between writers—here, men—and fairy tales. What makes the book new and revolutionary is that men are asked to speak about their love for fairy tales, and that they do. I saw my role as editor to be that of devotee, to support the writers in finding their form, the existential direction, of their contribution. I had many late-night conversations with authors about fairy tales, and in some ways I see this collection as a way for the reader to listen to a diverse dialogue about what fairy tales mean to our lives.

What these writings have in common is that each feels private. The essays are private, first and foremost, because the authors decided what they wanted to do with the request to write a "personal essay" about fairy tales. Rather than ask the writers questions that would force them to think about fairy tales through a particular lens—say, gender or childhood—I wanted instead to let them make their own way through the literature, in order to see what connections became revealed. For lack of a better word, I wanted to allow for a *natural* evolution of this new conversation. So I consider these writings to be very private, and I think readers will notice this in a number of ways, most prominently in the diversity of forms contained here and in the essays' intimate themes.

I was led by conversations with some contributors to expect essays about how boys felt left out of the tales—yet I got nary an essay addressing this theme. The closest to that subject came from Joshua Beckman, whose essay reads like a little prose poem about what little he knows about fairy tales—but reveals a lot more. It seems as if the writers went beyond their initial consideration to a much fuller place. Several writers possessively "requested" certain tales—"It's my favorite, I'll only write if *I'm* the one who can write on this tale"—only to send me an essay on a completely different fairy tale that, in writing on the original one, revealed itself to be of much greater, and deeper, personal importance. The intimate significance of these essays sneaked up on the authors themselves.

Johannes Göransson's contribution, an elegant meditation on experimental Swedish poetry, is as much a personal response to fairy tales as Willy Vlautin's plain-spoken memory piece about his grandmother telling him stories when he was a kid. Both essays reflect the writers' primary reaction to the question of how fairy tales had affected their lives. For Göransson, a poet and translator, fairy tales comprise an intense poetics; for Vlautin, a novelist and musician whose books and songs are populated with broken-down characters, fairy tales remind him of anxieties and fears. Michael Martone's deeply patterned essay about fatherhood draws upon fairy-tale scenes for its telling and reveals in narrative the strange ache of time. While Robert Coover's essay takes a deliciously arch and allegorical tone, it too explores similar themes: myth and legend, commerce and death.

What I wonder at most—and what I will highlight for readers as one of the primary results of this editorial experiment—is that the essays fail wonderfully, fail beautifully, at offering easy answers to the question of men and fairy tales.

That is, the collection of essays I received did not lend itself to a subtitle such as "Men Write about Fairy Tales, Sexuality, Love, Childhood, Marriage, and Myth." In their unbridled approach they contradict each other (one writer disdained fairy tales for much of his life; another loved them passionately since he was a child). They introduce unusual connections to little-known tales, reinforcing my premise that the cultural script about men and fairy tales is as yet mainly unknown (two authors chose to write about "The Story of the Youth Who Went Forth to Learn What Fear Was"—not one of the most canonized German fairy tales in America but clearly of influence). I received essays about "Bluebeard," "Hansel and Gretel," and "Snow White," but they address the fairy tales in unpredictable ways; and I received revealing and important essays about *kitsune* and the *Mrs. Piggle-Wiggle* books, unpredictable texts for a collection like this.

Even when addressing subjects we might expect the authors in a collection of men on fairy tales to address, such as fathers and sons, the writing illuminates in new and original ways. Jirí Cêch's bawdy prose remembers the meandering fairy tales his father told him—as an entrance into a remembrance of mistresses past; in Greg Bills's careful narration, a son considers how fairy tales, particularly "Jack and the Beanstalk," may illuminate his father's relationship to his son being gay. "Fairy tales," Bills writes, "offered not only an unregulated sanctuary for creatures that could not exist in reality . . . but also for emotions that had no conceivable outlet into reality. I could not be a gay boy in a world where gay boys did not exist." Richard Siken's lyric and painful essay also considers a father: "My father is reading me this story, and sometimes it is just a story, and other times it is his story, his history, he is sharing a sadness with me." *"You are in terrible danger,"* Siken continues, "I am Hansel Triumphant." This conflation of danger, sadness, and triumph appears often in *Brothers and Beasts*—making a pattern but in each essay making one anew.

It is as if I had sent each writer instructions to first read Virginia Woolf's *A Room of One's Own,* which offers the explicit instruction to writers that "it is fatal to be a man or woman pure and simple; one must be woman-manly or man-womanly," that "the whole of the mind must lie wide open if we are to get the sense that the writer is communicating his experience with perfect fullness." This notion of the woman-manly or man-womanly works to describe the essays contained here—in that not one makes an argument about gender—but it also works well with fairy tales, where so much is, as Max Luthi describes it, "sublimated," collapsed. Not only do the real and unreal exist in tales on the same plane (i.e., one does not reach the magical world through a portal but rather is always already there), but boy and girl, mother and father, donkey and hare, tree and egg—they too exist all together.

While I appreciate the celebration, both in scholarship and in popular culture, of the strong female characters in fairy tales, I think that, first and foremost, our devotion to fairy tales is with "the whole of the mind" and not with our gender. Phrased differ-

ently, perhaps less controversially, it is clear that in both *Mirror,*
Mirror and *Brothers and Beasts* artistic fervor comes first—a fervor
begun in childhood with a fervor for reading. (I will, of course,
be interested in what those who study this book for use in their
scholarship on fairy tales and gender can glean from it.)

For me, there was nothing like reading fairy tales as a child. As
Maria Tatar points out in her lovely foreword, "When you read a
book as a child, it sends chills up your spine and produces somatic
effects that rarely accompany the reading experience of adults."
Jack Zipes, in his afterword, writes, "The fairy tale has not been
partial to one sex or the other." Reading fairy tales—or writing
about them—is, I can assure you, one of the few ways adults can
re-create that delicious, somatic childhood chill.

Yet men, so discouraged from speaking personally about fairy
tales and their connection to them, may lose that opportunity—
which is a loss for us all. That is why I wanted so badly to do this
book. I was surprised by the urgency the writers felt too. And I
cherish the tenderness with which these writers talk about thim-
bles and flowers, myth makers and cowards, bears both little and
big. It is the tenderness that strikes me, the tenderness and the
urgency here.

As editor, I must thank Angela Carter, whose eclectic and dazzling editorial approach produced such magical volumes cele-
brating unknown stories with transformative power. Her novelist's eye allowed her to gather such special tales, stories that only
she had the goodness to see when others blithely ignored them. So
I thank Angela Carter for paving the way for those of us who also
wish to save fairy tales, in whatever small fashion we can.

I've arranged these essays in alphabetical order so you might
read them as you wish—to go where it is that you want to go, just
as I remember leafing through those huge fairy-tale books as a
child. As Luthi writes so eloquently in *Once Upon a Time: On the*
Nature of Fairy Tales, in fairy tales "loud talk and startled or threatening silence stand side by side, yet words of consolation also are
not wanting . . . the fairy tale is a universe in miniature." A little alphabetical universe.

One can, of course, read the works from beginning to end. One might wish to scan the annotated table of contents to get a feel for the pieces, and choose one that, in its opening sentences gathered there, catches the mood of the reader in that very moment. If one is looking for essays that take a more philosophical tone, or a more confessional tone, that is—these qualities are generally apparent in the table of contents. Likewise, as to the mode of expression (lyric, minimalist, grandiose) these too are revealed there. As editor, I can add that these essays very much lend themselves to re-reading; I find that each reveals something about the others.

I must, in closing, thank Donald Haase and Kathy Wildfong at Wayne State University Press for their kindness and for their belief in this book. And thank you to Maria Tatar and Jack Zipes for writing the foreword and afterword, and for so many years of patient goodwill—for welcoming me as wanderer into the world of fairy-tale scholarship, a magical place. And thank you, my generous contributors, for taking the path of needles and pins—for taking the risk to be here.

I know many writers who say that the memory of reading fairy tales is their first, and sometimes only, memory of *rapture*. I hope that this unpredictable, intense collection inspires you to read fairy tales—and then to read them again.

Steve Almond

AN INVESTIGATION OF THE AUTO-CURATIVE IMPULSE
AS IT RELATES TO DEPRIVATION AND TRAUMA IN
YOUNG SUBJECTS, or HOW MRS. PIGGLE-WIGGLE
HELPED ME SURVIVE CHILDHOOD

"All good fairy tales have meaning on many levels," Bruno Bettle-
heim observes in *The Uses of Enchantment.* "Only the child can
know which meanings are of significance to him at the moment."

So I think I should begin by telling you a little about the household I grew up in, which was, to all outward appearances, a hope-
ful place on a quiet suburban street with two industrious parents
and three bright, healthy boys, but which was, for its inhabitants
(at least for this one, though I would warrant all five of us), something closer to a house of horrors.

My parents were both eldest children, born into families of Jew-
ish ambition. They met at Yale Medical School, married in their
midtwenties, and had three children before they had completed
their residencies. My older brother, Dave, was born in 1964; my
twin brother, Mike, and I came along two years later.

We eventually settled on the south side of Palo Alto, California.
The city would later become synonymous with Silicon Valley
and its attendant prosperity. But the neighborhood we grew up in
was modest, a place of ranch homes and low-income apartment
houses.

Our parents were psychiatrists by profession and hippies by
moral inclination. They protested the war in Vietnam, took us to
live for a summer on a commune, made huge batches of homemade

jam, and worked at a therapeutic collective. They were noble people who did their best as citizens and parents. But they were overmatched by circumstances: too many children too quickly, too many expectations, not enough time for themselves or their children. The pervasive feeling in the home was one of deprivation. Nobody got enough. Nobody would ever get enough.

This bred a certain competitive anguish among us boys, a vicious need for recognition combined with an inability to accept praise, a tendency to withhold love from others and ourselves. We brutalized one another, physically and emotionally, and punished our parents by banishing them from our private kingdom.

For the most part they didn't know what to do with us.

I can remember our mother coming home from work to find the floor-length window off the kitchen shattered. Dave and I had been playing basketball indoors and crashed into the thing, diving for a loose ball. She gazed at the shards with a look I took at the time to be sadness but that I can now see was closer to surrender.

It was into this setting that Mrs. Piggle-Wiggle made her bustling entrance. Our mother read us the stories initially. Later, I read them to myself, often alone and by flashlight. I became a bit of a junkie, which was a curious and faintly embarrassing thing to be back when I was ten.

For the uninitiated, *Mrs. Piggle-Wiggle* was written by Betty MacDonald and originally was published in 1947. The stories in the original volume (three more would follow) are not fairy tales in the traditional sense. They do not traffic in symbolism or the supernatural. On the contrary, they are more like suburban morality plays. Mrs. Piggle-Wiggle herself is a kind of neighborhood witch doctress, an eccentric widow who lives in an upside-down house and befriends only children.

The plot of the standard Mrs. Piggle-Wiggle story runs like this: A child is misbehaving. His mother, having exhausted traditional modes of discipline, calls Mrs. Piggle-Wiggle, who calmly diagnoses the problem and recommends a cure.

Hubert Prentiss, for example, refuses to pick up his toys. Mrs. Piggle-Wiggle instructs his mother to leave him be. At first Hubert is thrilled. But soon his toys stack up so high he can't get out of his room. Eating becomes a problem: "After dinner Hubert's father tied the hose to the rake and held it up while Hubert put his mouth to the window opening and tried to get a drink of water." He gets a few drops, along with a crust of old bread smeared with peanut butter.

Then he receives a note inviting him to the circus and he panics. "Hubert began to cry and to try and kick his way to the door, but everything he kicked seemed to hit back," MacDonald writes. "He could hear the music of the circus parade growing fainter and fainter and so he bawled louder and louder."

He never fails to pick up his toys again.

Allen, a slow eater, tiny-bite taker, is cured by the same indulgence. Mrs. Piggle-Wiggle gives his mother several sets of dishes, each daintier than the one before: "The next day his mother brought out the small dishes. On the silver dollar plate she put three cornflakes, a piece of bacon the size of a snowflake, and a quarter of a teaspoon of egg. In the thimble cup she put ten drops of cocoa."

Allen is soon so weak he can barely drag himself to the table. When he tries to ride Mrs. Piggle-Wiggle's pony, he falls to the ground and lies there "like a wet sock, bawling."

The plot arcs were not particularly innovative. Why, then, did I find the stories so hypnotic? Because they offered a direct correspondence to my life. They were about troubled children learning to control their worst impulses in the face of well-meaning but ineffectual mothers and friendly but absent fathers. And they offered a powerful fantasy, particularly for the child of two therapists: that the key to recovery lies within the child himself.

Another example: Dick Thompson is described as a charming, intelligent child. But he is terribly selfish. As the story opens, his mother gives him fifty peppermint sticks to distribute to the neighborhood kids. Not only does he refuse to share them, but he cracks one girl on the hand with his baseball bat.

Mrs. Piggle-Wiggle gives Dick a Selfishness Kit that includes two dozen padlocks of various sizes (one as small as a penny), an array of labels, and, most enticingly, a pastry bag that, when filled with frosting, can be used to label his food. Dick labels everything from his dog to his school lunch. He's ecstatic for a few days. Then the other kids grow sick of his routine and begin to mock him, rather savagely, until he sees the error of his ways.

I remember this story in particular because I too struggled with selfishness as a kid. (My way of responding to feelings of deprivation was to hide my Halloween candy at the bottom of my dirty clothes hamper.)

I also remember a particular passage in which Dick's mother talks with Mrs. Piggle-Wiggle on the phone.

"Do you like Dick," she asks, anxiously, "in spite of his selfishness?"

"Of course I do," Mrs. Piggle-Wiggle says. "I love all children, but it distresses me when I see a child who has a disease like Selfishness or Answerbackism or Won't-Put-Away-Toys-itis and his parents don't do a thing to cure him."

As an adult I can see this attitude as perhaps a bit on the pathologizing side. But as a kid I felt reassured: Misbehavior didn't render children unlovable. It was only a matter of scrubbing their naughtiness away.

There were other reasons I worshipped the Mrs. Piggle-Wiggle stories. MacDonald had a knack for coining some of the strangest names in modern letters: Guinevere Gardenfield, Prunella Brown, Cormorant Broomrack, and (my personal fave) Paraphernailia Grotto. She was also deceptively witty. Embedded in each of the tales were little moments of comic genius.

After her kids refuse to go to bed at the assigned hour, a certain Mrs. Gray, for instance, calls her friend Mrs. Grassfeather. Mrs. Grassfeather reports that her husband "not only allows the children to stay up until 9:30 but he pays them as well for listening to Uncle Jasper while he goes to bed." The kids are very good about bedtime, Mrs. Grassfeather reports. "They know that if they whine and complain I will not let them stay up the next time Uncle Jasper comes over, which is about four nights a week."

A bit later in this story the Gray children, Bobby, Larry, and Susan, indulge in a midnight snack. "They ate about ten little sandwiches, a small dish of salted nuts, two little dishes of candy, some olives and pickles and some chocolate marshmallow cake." This bounty *amazed* me, as did the notion of children who could eat whatever they liked.

This was one of the most enticing aspects of MacDonald's nameless postwar suburb: the mothers were constantly baking cakes and cookies and serving them to their children when they returned from school. For a latch-key kid who self-medicated with sweets, it sounded like paradise.

And yet MacDonald's vision of childhood was anything but bright and sunny. As should be clear, she understood that children were capable of extreme cruelty and solipsism. And her cures were drastic, often bordering on kinky.

The example that leaps to mind is the Radish Cure, which is administered to a girl named Patsy, who refuses to take a bath. Mrs. Piggle-Wiggle explains it thusly: "Let Patsy strictly alone, as far as washing is concerned, for several weeks. When she has about half an inch of rich black dirt all over her and after she is asleep at night, scatter radish seeds on her arms and head. Press them in gently and then just wait. I don't think you will have to water them because we are in the rainy season now and she probably will go outdoors now and then. When the little radish plants have three leaves you may begin pulling the largest ones."

"Oh yes," Mrs. Piggle-Wiggle adds, "Patsy will probably look quite horrible before the cure is over, so if you find that she is scaring too many people or her father objects to having her around, let me know and I will be glad to take her over here. You see all of my visitors are children and it doesn't frighten them."

I feel duty bound to report here—with a certain reluctance—the nickname my brothers gave me as a child: Stinkpot. I'm not sure how I earned this sobriquet, but it had the intended effect of making me terribly self-conscious about my personal hygiene.

Of all the Mrs. Piggle-Wiggle stories, the one with the most immediate (and enduring) significance concerned Anne and Joan Russell, twins who are perpetually quarreling. I needn't belabor the similarities here. What's important is the attitude the story expresses toward the girls: "In the first place, fighting and quarreling are merely habits," Mrs. Piggle-Wiggle explains. "They wake up and begin shouting rudely at each other. It soon becomes a habit and they forget how to be courteous." Her solution is simple: the parents must imitate their children, until the twins "see themselves as others see them."

In the gentle world of Mrs. Piggle-Wiggle, the naughty twins immediately recognize the error of their ways. And I can still recite, practically by heart, the passage that ends the story, as in many ways it represents the precise wish fantasy I harbored for most of my childhood: "Daddy said, 'I'll tell you what we'll do. We'll all join hands and solemnly pledge that there shall be no more quarreling in this house. Then, we'll all walk up to Findley's Drugstore and seal the pledge with ice cream. Does everyone agree?'"

How I longed for such an outcome! A pact of mutual surrender sealed in hot fudge, an end to the violent bickering and fortified anguish.

I probably don't need to tell you that my own parents actually tried this same gambit on several occasions. It never worked.

The kids ministered to by Mrs. Piggle-Wiggle, after all, lived in households where love was openly, if somewhat ineptly, expressed. Children who misbehaved had merely picked up a bad habit.

Of course, the destructive impulses within children are not merely habits. They are manifestations of fear and aggression, thwarted love that has been distorted into evil. So I knew better. But I suppose that's why we turn to fairy tales. We wish to see our traumas conquered.

It should be noted that Betsy MacDonald wrote three additional Mrs. Piggle-Wiggle books. Her later editions never captured me in the same way. The cures in these books consist mostly of magic pills and potions, an eerie forerunner of today's psychopharmocopia. In one volume, Mrs. Piggle-Wiggle has moved to a ranch, which serves as a kind of halfway house for various young miscreants.

That wasn't what I was looking for. I didn't want to have to take a pill or leave home. I wanted the intervention of some powerful maternal figure who could help my brothers and me withstand the shame of self-recognition.

It never happened in real life (lord knows), but it did happen every time I read *Mrs. Piggle-Wiggle.*

Brian Baldi

CLEVER HANS

The first thing I do is make arrangements to drag a slice of bacon around town by a rope. From my local grocer I choose a package of thick-cut, streaky rashers. Durability seems to be the issue here, but the slice must also be singular and with bold contours. The reason: I want the bacon to be noteworthy. With this in mind, I fry up the entire package in my kitchen, and choose for my act the most articulated slice—a nicely browned one with defined flashes of fat and nicely scalloped edges. It is the perfect strip of bacon to drag around town by a rope.

This undertaking, it should be mentioned, has been recommended to me through a reading of the Grimms' tale "Clever Hans." In this sly, dialogue-driven story a boy named Hans makes six visits to a girl named Gretel. Each time she asks, "What have you brought me?" Each time, Hans replies ineloquently, "Brought nothing. You give something." He is a simple boy, this Hans. Luckily for him, though, Gretel shows a tremendous capacity for putting up with his lack of expressiveness and abundance of demands. On each visit she promptly relinquishes an item to him. A needle, a knife, a young goat, a piece of bacon, a calf, and finally she hands over herself. None of these items are handled well by Hans. The needle he transports home in a pile of hay. When his mother tells him he has been foolish, and that he should have kept the needle in his sleeve, Hans puts the next item, a knife, in his sleeve. And like that he continues to apply his mother's last instruction to the next item he receives. After being told he should have transported a young goat by tying a rope around its neck, Hans then ties a rope around a slice of bacon given to him by Gretel and drags it home. Dogs eat it on the way.

Literalism besets him, or so it seems. One startling thing about "Clever Hans" is that it is not entirely clear from the tale *why* Hans behaves the way he does. Does he consider himself an early performance artist? Does he like to torment his mother and Gretel with aberrant behavior? Or does he suffer from some sort of contextual aphasia? He speaks with phenomenally dumb economy and without much analysis ("What have you done with the calf, Hans?" "Put it on head, kicked face"), suggesting that the story may be an itemized parable about the perils of unnuanced thinking.

I'm not terribly concerned with any edifying purpose in the tale, though. It seems to me that when a boy who transports a calf on his head gets kicked in the face, an unsurprising commentary is being made. Same with the leashed bacon. What interests me, however, is the world of metaphor upon which all writing depends. Not just metaphor in the sense of the literary mechanism one is taught about in school. I mean the entire world that imaginative writing enables. As the poet and critic Susan Stewart has written, "By abstraction, the metaphor presents another domain of meaning that is more than the sum of its component parts." Or, put another way, imaginative writing opens up a new space where readers can be limber, hazard their own routes, and make new associations and extrapolations about life. In the case of Hans somehow he's found himself in a literary setting where conversation is clipped, goats can be placed in pockets, and events come in an absurd, progressive, climactic order. This is the quintessential metaphor space of the tale, but all other forms of imaginative writing create their useful fields of connotation too.

Fair enough, but what happens when the metaphor world is made real? What varied, blossoming insights can be gained by bringing something over from the other side of the fictional divide? Do the fabrications and associations caused by the realm of imaginative writing have the same kick and waggle when their instigating act of fiction is imported to the physical world? For example, if a man could actually be transformed into an insect, would his dilemma have the same effect on us as it does in fiction? Or, what could be gleaned from actually falling in love in an actual time of cholera? These questions seem relevant to the whole enterprise of artistic creation, and that is why a rasher of bacon must be tied to a rope.

At my local hardware store the employees wear blue vests and stand chatting in the aisles. One taps the toe of his boot against a fifty-pound bag of rock salt. Another rests the palm of his hand on top of a paint-can pyramid. Nearly everyone speaks through a mustache and seems overburdened by the length of the day. Down one aisle I am trying to choose between the virtues of two ropes. The first is made from natural fibers, promises to hold knots securely, has some "natural stretch," and is biodegradable. The second, made from nylon, boasts "built-in stretch for shock absorption" and is long lasting. While I am certainly tempted by the prospect of my bacon benefiting from shock absorption, I choose the natural strand of rope. My project will undoubtedly gain from the fidelity of natural ingredients. A young employee walks by, perhaps the only one in the store younger than fifty, and I ask him to cut off an eight-foot length for me.

"I'm going to do something very unusual with this rope," I say flatly.

The employee does not respond, perhaps guessing at an untoward intention he'd rather not consider.

"I'm going to drag bacon with it."

He turns to me. "Bacon?"

"Yeah, it's for a project."

He seems satisfied with this answer, nods, and begins to measure out the rope. He toggles a switch on the wall that heats up a thin strip of metal held by an electrified clamp. The metal strip gets red-hot, and he presses the strand against it. Smoke bubbles from the rope, which is cut and cauterized at the same time. "Here you go," he says, and, like that, I have amassed the two things necessary to bring part of a Grimms' tale to life.

My first inclination is to make sure the imaginative world of metaphor is made physical without still being an obvious metaphor. Put another way, I want people to encounter through happenstance the act of my dragging a rasher of bacon around town and find meanings on their own without trying to guess at mine. Which is, of course, impossible. In our society, dragging bacon is not generally something one does without some sort of agenda. But at the very least I figure I won't call attention to myself with strange clothing. I will just be a lone man out on a walk. Now, I will admit this idea has some appeal to me beyond the utility of putting the metaphorical world to test. I like the notion of strolling through town in my wool coat, nodding to passersby with a hail-fellow-well-met attitude (but not too zealously), admiring the church steeples (but not too noticeably), looking into the windows of a chocolate shop (but not too keenly), feeling confident, and pulling behind me a strip of pork that wriggles and jumps at every bump of the sidewalk. Negations of expectation like this offer a nice release from the everyday grammar of living, but the point here is to make an instance of fiction come to life in the everyday world, so I decide to tone it down a bit. Act normal. Seem almost bored.

There is another thing I must admit about trying to reenact fiction: the context of my town is different from the context of a Grimms' tale. The denizens of my small New England town, when seeing me and my bacon, do not have the benefit of preceding events that can explain what's happening. Instead of having a feel for the repetition and contours of the written story, they will likely have a cup of coffee in one gloved hand and may have exited a local shop. Maybe they have just purchased some soap made from shea butter and verbena, or a droll, politically minded refrigerator magnet. This is very different from what happens in "Clever Hans," but the point is to import one instance of the metaphorical world, not put on a full theatrical reenactment. The bacon will suffice.

There is a dread wind that requires me to button my coat shut. Sitting on the steps of the local church, I tie a hackneyed slipknot around the bacon until it seems secure and then, after a deep breath, begin to keelhaul it up and down the most populated part of my town.

And how does metaphor fare when made real? Not very well. As it turns out, people do not like to see a helpless curlicue of bacon dragged around. It bothers them. They may find it purposeful and intriguing in a book, but when a young man strolls around with some pork on a leash, that's a different story altogether. Many people, upon seeing me, pretend not to see me. I have arranged to have a friend observe the event by following behind me discretely, and she later tells me that numerous people take a keen interest in the bacon being dragged but purposely avoid getting too close to the metaphorical incident. They point and laugh. They make efforts to avoid me. Anticipating such a response, I approach people and ask them for their interpretation of the event. "You'll notice that I am dragging behind me, on the end of this rope, a slice of bacon," I say. "What are your thoughts on this?" A man looking for spare change tells me it should be used in a sandwich. A postal worker tells me it looks like I am trying to catch a dog. Another man tells me he isn't quite sure what I'm doing but says, "My dog would have a very concrete idea what to do right now." Another man, a tidy dresser with an aggressive bearing, indicts my sanity. These interpretations can be seen to represent the context of the person making them. Just like different readers may interpret "Clever Hans" differently. But, still, these people are all addressing the immediate practicalities of the situation. When I ask them if the dragged bacon can teach them any lessons, or help them to realize something new about the condition of life, they all say no, not really, and walk off. They have little interest in the figurative value of my act. When asked if the bacon itself calls forth some association, or if the act would have a different significance if I were to be dragging, say, a wristwatch, they still admit nothing. "No, not really," they say. Or: "I don't know." Abstracted, correlative thinking does not seem to appeal to the citizens of my town on an ordinary Tuesday. Not only that, the full reenactment of the bacon-dragging section in "Clever Hans" is hindered by some very unhelpful dog owners. One man, upon seeing the meat behind me, yanks at his dog's leash, preventing his canine from taking my bacon. I ask another man whether his dogs are allowed to eat bacon, and he tells me that he doesn't think it would be a very good idea.

I am about to give up on the intellectual resonance of dragging bacon across town when I hear the conversation of two young women walking behind me, both in their late teens by the sound of it. I slow my pace to ensure that they see and have time to form opinions about my rope and bacon. This is a tactic I have developed—a few moments for a hasty impression, then a few more for a well-considered one. After about twenty paces I turn around and introduce my intellectual undertaking. "You may notice that I am trailing behind me a piece of bacon," I say. The girls stop walking. One is wearing a light ski jacket, the other a sweatshirt and pink, mirrored aviator glasses. We all stare at the piece of bacon on the sidewalk. They give it a long, generous look.

"Does this act of dragging bacon call forth any ideas in you?" I finally ask.

"Well, it kind of reminds me of those foam dragons you can buy at the state fair," one of them says, "the ones that walk behind you on a leash when you pull them."

"Yeah," says the other one. "It *is* like that!"

"You're right," I admit, "It's very much like that."

They look at it some more. I have their full absorption in this matter.

"I shouldn't tell you this," I continue, "but this is a literary re-enactment."

"Oh." It is an *oh* of intrigue. No one takes an eye off the bacon.

"Is there anything you think you can learn from seeing me drag this piece of bacon around town?"

"Well, I wouldn't judge anyone, that's for sure," one says.

"Yeah," says the other, "I think people judge too much already."

"So you have no problem with me and my bacon?"

"Nope."

"Thank you very much."

The girls walk on, resuming their conversation. They have considered the realm of the rope and bacon, they have likened it to other circumstances in their lives, and they have made a decision as to their relationship to the matter at hand. And then they turn the corner.

Back at the church steps I reel in the bacon and loop the strand of rope like a cowboy's lariat. It would be presumptuous to think that by attempting to reify one portion of the metaphor in "Clever Hans," I have reified the usefulness of literary metaphor spaces. One pair of lingering teenagers, however encouraging their efforts may be at contemplating how dragging bacon relates to their perception of life, does not make a mass movement toward big-hearted conceptual thinking. But they have introduced me to at least one useful notion: It's a shame that we don't more actively use the quotidian as an opportunity to create metaphorical spaces. That we don't bust our moorings. That we don't see cities in our muffins and ourselves in the leaf piles. If we did, the relations we might make from one mental domain to the next, the innumerable crossings and recrossings, the bringing of fresh pies, the borrowing of cups of sugar, would certainly increase, and who knows what else with them. More empathy seems likely, perhaps also understanding.

I can't say that it worked out well for Hans. By gouging out the eyes of some sheep and then hucking them at Gretel at the end of his tale, he succeeds, predictably, only in chasing her away. And if a person runs away at the end of a two-and-a-half page story, well, that's final as far as that text goes. But not for the reader. The reader can continue making associations, extrapolating, revisiting the paths and places, and making real-life applications. As for me, it remains to be seen whether or not there are any long-term civic repercussions to traversing the barrier between metaphorical spheres and actual life using bacon. That tale is still upon its time.

Christopher Barzak

THE BOY WHO WENT FORTH

Once upon a time there was a boy who read fairy tales. He was a readerly child born into a family that did not read for pleasure. Not his father, not his two older brothers, not his mother. The only reading material that made its way into the hands of his family was the newspaper or magazines. He was not the sort of boy who found much use in the newspaper, though, or in his mother's *Women's World* issues, or in his father's *Deer Hunter* subscription. Instead he preferred books full of fantastic occurrences that would never be found among the weather predictions and accident reports of the news or mixed in among the recipes for ambrosia, diet fads, advertisements for crossbows, and personal narratives of deer hunting in the mountains of West Virginia, all of which were available in magazines his parents purchased. No one commented upon his peculiar reading habit for a long time because the books he brought home from the school library kept him out of the way, and because of this the early years of his childhood were very happy.

Like that boy, I grew up reading in a home where no one read, and in that home where my older brothers (had they read) wouldn't have been caught dead with a Charles Perrault book, I grew up reading fairy tales. I was an anomaly, I think, born in a small rural town in Ohio, in a ranch house my father built on my grandparents' farm. Looking back on my childhood and adolescence, recalling the friends of my youth, I remember being aware at a young age that, among the boys I was friends with, none of them read very much. And they especially didn't read fairy tales. Watching the Disney versions was okay when we were small, but even those became off-limits the nearer we drew to our teenage years.

And yet I counted fairy tales among my varied reading pleasures. I enjoyed comic books (Marvel rather than DC), mysteries (Poe), adventure stories for boys (Craig's *My Side of the Mountain*), science fiction and fantasy (Le Guin's Earthsea cycle), horror (again Poe), folktales (Irving), and fairy tales (Perrault rather than the Grimms, though I love the Grimms as well as Andersen). I didn't speak of my reading habits with my friends or family. It was private. When I read, I felt as if I could leave the world around me where—perhaps I knew even then, in some corner of my mind— I didn't quite fit. Why would I expose the very activity that allowed me to engage in a kind of freedom, that allowed me access to a world in which the limitations of this one disappeared and my imagination could roam past the boundaries of the life I'd been born into? I did not hide my reading, as that would only have aroused suspicion, but I did not speak about it either. I must also make clear, though, that I didn't know I was protecting something. I didn't realize that until I was older.

Although I loved reading fairy tales, there was a certain kind of fairy tale I hated to discover. Tales in which two or three sons and a father act as the central characters, wherein one or two of the boys are either talented, smart, handsome, or all of these things, and the youngest or third son is a weak, strange, malformed, or stupid creature. I took an immediate dislike to these stories, but at the time I wasn't sure why. When I came across fairy tales that used this pattern of characters, though, I would pass these stories over for tales in which someone's dreams come true.

What I did not understand then was that I had found a type of fairy tale that reflected some aspect of myself, my family, my experience in the "real world," and what it reflected I did not want to see. I sought out the fairy tales that did not reflect my experience, because I didn't want to find myself in stories that were not reaffirming about my placement in the world. What the strange brothers of fairy tales showed me was that, in my family, I was this sort of child. The weakling, the strange thinker, the one set apart from social normality.

Take the Grimm Brothers' "The Story of the Youth Who Went Forth to Learn What Fear Was," which begins with this opening:

> A certain father had two sons, the elder of whom was smart and sensible, and could do everything, but the younger was stupid and could neither learn nor understand anything, and when people saw him they said, "There's a fellow who will give his father some trouble!"

Some fairy tales deliver meaning in an intricate web of symbols that need to be decoded at a subconscious level. But in many of the tales about sons and brothers, there is not much necessity for decoding. The conflict within the story is spread out immediately before the eyes of the reader within the first sentence. There was a father who had two sons, one who was sensible, the other stupid, and the stupid one is going to cause a lot of trouble for the father, isn't he? The situation is then set into motion when the father compares the stupid son with his smart brother, who earns his own wages:

> Now it came to pass that his father said to him one day "Hearken to me, thou fellow in the corner there, thou art growing tall and strong, and thou too must learn something by which thou canst earn thy living. Look how thy brother works, but thou dost not even earn thy salt." "Well, father," he replied, "I am quite willing to learn something—indeed, if it could but be managed, I should like to learn how to shudder. I don't understand that at all yet." The elder brother smiled when he heard that, and thought to himself, "Good God, what a blockhead that brother of mine is! He will never be good for anything as long as he lives. He who wants to be a sickle must bend himself betimes."

During the story the stupid son, on a mission to learn what fear is, unwittingly breaks the leg of a minister who attempts to frighten him by pretending to be a ghost in a bell tower of the church. The boy then spends the night among the hanging corpses of the dead husbands of a rope maker's daughter without realizing he is keeping company with dead men, and he destroys demonic cats in a haunted castle because he knows they are tricking him when they ask if he wants to play cards (slyly he says yes, and before they can put forth their claws, he destroys them). He conquers an entire haunted castle full of ghosts and demons and the living dead. Yet somehow this boy is considered stupid.

The real trick of this tale is in what it reveals about the teller of the story, who I take to be a great big sort of Everyman or Everywoman figure, a member of small-town agrarian society who understands the rules of that society and what is considered good and what is considered bad. We are told that the second son is stupid because he has no way of earning his own bread, and because he apparently does not fear many of the things that everyone else in the society clearly sees reason to fear. He is unafraid of corpses, ghosts, and demons. He does not run when anyone with any sense would run. Of course the town and the town teller, Mr. or Mrs. Everyman or Everywoman, finds the boy to be a stupid, queer sort of fellow.

Difference, then, constitutes stupidity in the land of fairy tales. When I first read these stories, I was too tender to the sting of the word *stupid* and how the town members and family members of the "stupid" sons treated them so cruelly. Later in my life, in my teenage years and while I was in college, did not my own father tell me—using almost exactly the same words as the father of the boy who went forth to learn about fear—that I would have to figure out a way to earn my salt in this world? I was not unaware of my difference from my brothers. I had continued reading once I was past childhood and the early years of adolescence. I was interested in foreign languages and cultures and intellectual ideas. I wanted to go to college. My oldest brother had gone to college for a semester and found it wanting, then took a technical degree that enabled him to sell insurance. He's very happily selling insurance to this day. My middle brother didn't attempt college at all. He's worked in a factory since graduating from high school. Yet I was the one who was often spoken to as being useless or lazy because the things in which I had an interest were not socially understood within the context of a working-class family. Why did I not seek out manual labor or a quick degree that would allow me to do some sort of lower-level white-collar job like my brothers'? Why, asked my aunt—my father's sister—on the phone one night, did I stay in my room all the time reading book after book? My mother defended me to others but in private would occasionally try to sway me to try wanting things others could understand. I think she loved me for my differences yet also wondered why I couldn't make my differences somehow more acceptable to everyone. Why couldn't I make them more of a quirk, for example, instead of something so essential about my being?

When I was seventeen and about to graduate from high school, my mother took me around to various hospitals to apply for admittance to their X-ray technology programs, which would have made me an X-ray technologist after a year or two of on-the-job training and classes. I nearly was admitted but for the good graces of an interviewer who sensed that I perhaps was too young to make this decision. She told me that I could do the program but she felt I should attend college for a year first; if I still wanted to be an X-ray technologist after that, I could apply the following year. I was secretly relieved that this plan didn't work out and entered a community college the following fall. I was supposed to major in nursing (my family said I should at least study something useful), but secretly I changed my major to English within the first few weeks of my first semester.

To my family, many of the decisions I was making with my life seemed senseless and even stupid, and for a long time I thought perhaps that I was stupid too (for the first two years of college I avoided being called on in class because I thought anything I said would be inadequate, whereas I later discovered I had some interesting ideas when I was drawn out by a professor who told me I had talent). But like the boy who went forth to learn fear, I continued on my path undeterred, making the choices that made sense to me, even when they made sense to no one from the world I grew up in. "Aren't you afraid of how you will support yourself one day?" my parents and family members often said. In private my mother continued occasionally in her attempts to persuade me to be more realistic. "Writing is a good hobby," she once told me, "but you need to be able to do more than that in this world, Christopher."

I understand that they truly worried and cared about my seemingly senseless choices because they had no template that would show them any real way in which books and writing could be of any practical use to me as an adult. And I had no template for this route in life either. I often thought perhaps they were right and I was being a complete fool, like the boy who went forth to learn what fear was, but like that boy I kept going my own way.

It was not until I re-read as an adult the Grimms' fairy tales, as well as Hans Christian Andersen's and Charles Perrault's stories, that I came to understand why the stories of the dullard sons and brothers pierced me so keenly as a child, to the point that I would slap a book closed immediately or flip furiously to find a different sort of tale. As an adult I was able to see that the stupid sons were stupid only in the eyes of constructed social norms, that they were not inherently useless or strange. That they were, in many cases, the real heroes of their lives and of the lives of their families. From Perrault's Tom Thumb, a tiny weakling among his healthy strong brothers, I learned that the smallest, weakest child could also be the one to outwit an ogre and save his brothers from certain death and his family from poverty. His smallness, his weakness, provided him with advantages and a keen intelligence that his brothers did not have.

But it is to the Brothers Grimm boy who went forth to learn what fear was that I still return. As an adult male reader of fairy tales, I can now take some comfort and nourishment from his absurd journey, his going forth fearlessly on a path that others would turn away from. In him I've found a sort of kindred spirit; I've seen a sort of metaphor for some aspects of my experience in this world. I no longer slap the book shut when I come across a story about a stupid son or brother. Instead I read on, fearlessly, so that I can discover how they become who they are meant to become, which is what we all are meant to do in our brief lives in this world, whether anyone else understands the way we're walking or not.

Joshua Beckman

THE LITTLE I KNOW ABOUT FAIRY TALES

At times there are bears. Often there are sisters. In the evening there is darkness and in the daytime there is light. I know that there are apples, and I know that there are breadcrumbs, and I know that there is porridge. I know that one must eat, and I know that one must never ever eat what one is given. I know that the young despair of dying and that the old despair of living. I know that sound portends something to fear and silence equally so. I know that there is a private life of want among the animals unlike that which we attribute to them. I know that time and the body exist despite their frailty in dreams. I know that buildings are empty or full, and that whatever can reflect will reflect. I know there are sacks and boxes and buckets. I know that gardens are mysterious. I know that human triumph is never fully redemptive. I know that recollected in the air are all the told stories of all time, each taking up a little space, and I know, despite everything, that the end, when it comes, is almost always the end.

Greg Bills

JACK AND THE GIANT

Jack longed for the Giant. Before there was a beanstalk—when the boy still lacked even the Idea of a Beanstalk—Jack lay in bed and looked out his window at the sky, dreaming of a cloud castle and the man inside it.

What Jack wanted from the Giant is a matter for debate; it is doubtful that Jack himself could have said. Jack was not an introspective fellow. As subsequent events would show, Jack was impulsive. Jack was daring, the antithesis of prudent. Jack was both heroically minded and something of a fool. Entrusted by his mother with the family's sole material possession, their cow, Jack would quickly trade off the elderly beast, their toehold in the ownership society, for a handful of beans. Magic beans, as it turned out, but there was no guarantee of their efficacy at the time of the transaction. Jack was operating from instinct. Sure, he was enticed by the canny hucksterism of the bean trader, but before a boy could be made to fall for that bill of goods, he would need to have some concept of what those beans might do for him, how he imagined this new venture might evolve.

So the Giant. Maybe Jack had no particular giant in mind; maybe it was just a giant-sized hole in his dreams and desires that the big-G Giant later came forward to fill. Then again, consider how this Giant's castle with all its riches—its chatty harp and gold-gravid goose—had chosen to orient itself in midair directly above Jack's mother's kitchen garden. When Jack's mother hurled the beans out the window in disgust, she couldn't have flung them far, no matter how good a pitch she had. And those beans were not the seed form of some creeping vine, some horizontal wanderer, an ivy or a kudzu; the stalks shot straight up. The castle must have been overhead already, waiting.

So Jack and the Giant. It is inconceivable that Jack hadn't noticed the place looming there. Casting its tarry shadow across the house as the sun passed behind it. Even if the suspended dwelling were as modest as the peasant hovel in which Jack and his mom were tenanted, its owner was a giant. A giant's hovel is still going to be pretty damn big. And it wasn't a hovel, it was a fucking castle! Suffice to say, it had not gone unnoticed by Jack. And people must have discussed it. Neighbors. Relatives. Friends. Hey, Jack, that . . . um . . . palace over your house. What's up with that? And before the time came for his own visit to the place, Jack had found himself fitted with an insider's knowledge of what among the inventory was ripest for pilfering: the goose, for instance, and not the goat or the chattering monkey in its cage. Clearly, people had briefed Jack. The word had got around.

It would be only logical to assume that there was an economic relationship here. Between the Giant's House and Jack's. The Master's Place and the Servants' Quarters. The Landlord and His Tenants. And it might be that Jack's flight of fancy, as he lay on his narrow cot and looked up through the window, was fueled by some righteous proletarian rage. One day, if I ever can get up there, there is going to be some serious redistribution of income around here. You hear me, Mr. Big Stuff? Maybe it was Jack's envy of all the finer things that such a palace must contain, all tantalizingly packaged yet beyond the reach of his upstretched arm. Except . . .

Except Jack never would show himself to be fiscally motivated. Sure, he would swap out Milky-White with her shriveled teats for a bunch of—whooo—magic beans and feel that he got the better end of things. And, sure, he might skedaddle with a golden goose when the possibility presented itself. But this opportunism is the casual greed of a child; it doesn't suggest any acumen. It is not as if, lying there, he was *planning* any of this. If he hadn't stumbled across the stranger with the beans, if his mother hadn't responded to his foolhardiness with a fit of pique—well—he would have remained on his back, staring up.

Could it be that he just wanted to look around? If there were a castle in the clouds above your house, you would have to wonder what it was like inside. And you would never get the chance to peek into the windows, unless . . . Unless, what? Some longings do not suggest even a fantasy of their fulfillment. If only I had a really, really huge beanstalk . . . Yeah, right.

And what if it was not the castle, or its accoutrements, but the Giant himself who was the source of Jack's fascination? What if he longed to reduce, somehow, the altitude between the Giant and himself? Jack may have pondered why the Giant had intentionally affixed himself to the sky overhead. It is worth noting that Jack had no father on the scene. Widowed, passersby would assume, seeing Jack's mom struggling along with Jack in their tiny house, reduced to selling off the livestock. But what if . . . What if Jack couldn't put into words the association between the Giant and himself that he was imagining? He might not be able to express it . . . but . . . Jack's mom and the Giant. Jack and the Giant. Even with a Parent Deceased, Jack would have some precedent to consider. Heaven—Up There—was one of those places where the inventory of the Dead and Gone was traditionally stored. Their bodies might be composting underground, rich loam for rooting beans. But their spirits—whatever remained of beings after they had eschewed their exterior husks—would spiral skyward. Plus, while enclosed in the seed of the flesh, there is a limitation of scale, but once the soul breaks clean, why not become gigantic? Was it, could it be, Jack's father up there—magnified, enormous?

The way some people told it, there was a Mrs. Giant, who was not, however, a giantess herself. Sometimes there was this wife. Sometimes there was not. Although she hardly seemed important. Maybe the Giant had left Jack's mom for Mrs. G; Jack might resent the substitution, take offense on his mother's behalf, but it didn't ultimately matter. What mattered to Jack was the Giant. Jack and the Giant.

... But it may be time to stop pretending that Jack's desires belong to anyone but me. In no iteration of Jack's tale does he show the least inclination toward reverie—over his parentage or any other subject. And because my parents never separated, the ambiguous provenance of the Giant's Wife is of no real interest to me. It is now time to stop speaking through Jack, living through Jack, playing around inside Jack, and confront the Giant myself. Greg and the Giant.

Oh, this is *hard*. To describe my first Dream of the Giant is to tip a pot of scalding shame and let it spill across my scalp and down my face. Shame, embarrassment, self-disgust: these are always the most assertive of feelings, more the Twinkies than the diamonds of sensory memory—always disconcertingly fresh. And this recollection of mine is also erotically charged. And an early one as well.

I was ... How old was I? I can't place this scene in time, although the details suggest I was three or younger. I was in my first bedroom with its dingy, matted yellow carpet and its red-painted shelves filled with toys. The door to the hall was closed, suggesting I recognized that this would be an activity requiring privacy. I stripped off my clothes and climbed naked into a long silky pillowcase. The case was a unique article that I had located in the hall linen closet, matching none of the bedding in any room of the house. Feet first, I snuggled into this cool slinky sack, curling my knees up to my chest after I touched the bottom, scrunching until my head was securely below the lip of the pillowcase. Then I imagined the Giant. With his huge hands and black beard. (My parents had a Kodak slide of a painted statue of Paul Bunyan with ax and ox that I loved to look at in the handheld slide viewer.) The Giant would lift the sack and sling it over his shoulder and carry it off with him over the hill. With me, quite helpless but unafraid, inside. That was the extent of the game. I remember repeating the procedure of entering the sack several times in succession—but solely on that afternoon, then never again. I don't know where the idea came from or where it went. I do remember the impression that I was being kidnapped, taken away from my family and everything

I knew, to live at the Giant's whim in some distant realm. And each time I climbed into the sack, I longed for the Giant to arrive and hoist my weight into the air and settle me against his back.

My shame here is not in the memory itself. I can see my child self acting with a solid intensity, without guile, with a pure craving. And my recollection of the event feels like simple fact: no different than a birthday party, a car trip up the winding road to the ruins at Mesa Verde, an image of fat bees darting among the raspberry canes alongside the house. It is in the telling that the moment seems soiled. It is in the admission that I was (still am) a naked boy dreaming of an encounter with a Giant.

Children, American children, are not allowed desire. It is not possible to suggest that playful things—rolling down a hill, racing through the sprinklers, lodging a running hose into the waistband of a swimsuit, slowing to sense the rasp of tall grass against exposed shins—are in any way aspects of the sensual life of a child. To suggest the sensual life of a child is to suggest the sensual mind of a child. To suggest a sensual, even sexual, willfulness in a child is to disrupt our culture's understanding of innocence. This vision of childhood innocence is pervasive and monolithic, and it is horribly susceptible to violation. (Do you feel the prickle of your hackles' being raised by the drift of this paragraph? I do. Are we being asked to imagine the existence of a sexualized child as some first move toward an embrace of child molestation? Isn't there something prurient in being asked to picture kids in swimsuits at play on a summer lawn? Why is the writer making this all so sordid when it is so totally, TOTALLY INNOCENT?) A child cannot have desire, an awareness or an erotics of the body, because our collective sense of childhood is too simplistic and fragile to absorb the possibility.

Oh, also, gay children do not exist. The wisdom goes that children are too unformed and vulnerable to be burdened with all this clattering of sexual identity. There are sissies and tomboys, sure, but a three-year-old lesbian? A six-year-old gay boy? What could it possibly mean to apply those terms to ones so young? Any envisioning of a gay preschooler would need, first, to clear the hurdle of imagining a sensual/sexual life for a child (see above for how well that works) and, second, to recognize how thoroughly gendered and heterosexualized the daily culture of a child already is. To locate the accepted viewpoint it is not necessary to look at the issue through the powerful and terrifying lens of sin and damnation that religious conservative teaching provides. It is sufficient to acknowledge the default setting of the mainstream: After all, we assume, *most* children are normal, most sissies and tomboys will grow out of it, so how necessary is it to accommodate the odd few? It might even be counterproductive, entrenching problems that would otherwise disappear with time. There *are* gay, lesbian, transgendered adults—we see that now, like it or not—and they start showing up in college, maybe even high school. But who can say where they came from? We will let those odd few boys and girls locate—without the support of family, friends, teachers, or culture—the self-awareness and the courage to reveal themselves, and then we will deal with them, supportively or not, as we see fit. There is nothing malicious in our attitude, nothing to reproach ourselves about. Simply, there *are* no gay children.

So. There I am in my pillowcase waiting for the Giant. And here I am in a land where children do not have a sensual life, where gay children do not exist, and where converging the topics of sexuality and childhood (even one's own) can cast a sweaty sheen of pedophilic intent over the discussion. Am I meant to return to that bedroom and that boy and tell him that he can't have wanted what he thought he wanted, that he didn't feel what he felt? Would it be better to assume it never happened? Or, if I must persist in believing my own memories, should I suspect that the moment is a residue of abuse, that my childhood innocence must have been influenced, interfered with?—But fuck this! I feel lucky to be angry enough to overcome the shame and suffocation. I *was* that boy, and I *did* get naked and climb into that pillowcase. And I *did* wait for the Giant to take me away with him.

Now something obvious needs to be stated about the Giant. Namely, *all* adults are giants in the eyes of young children. As we quickly grow, we forget that we once sat comfortably in a sock drawer. That we squeezed easily through the gap that neighborhood dogs had stretched into the chainlink fence. That we had to stand on a stool to reach the sink. All grown people loomed over us, leaving us in a realm of knees. Dress hems. Belt buckles. Purses. Adult conversation happened up there in the stratosphere, audible but distant, like a storm rumbling around the ceiling or the sky. Older siblings taffy-stretched up to this higher layer, although they might still reach down to our level to help or torment, according to their whim. (One of my brothers, twelve years my senior, used every opportunity to jump out at me from dark places; he once dangled me by the heels over the upper railing of a staircase; and I hated and feared him more than any fairy-tale ogre or movie monster.) Adults, with bodies vast as landscapes, were always present but also always somehow remote.

The Giant in my first Dream of the Giant was required to be a giant only to *me*. I did not imagine that he would stand me up on his palm, that he could slip me into his pocket. I believed that he would toss me over his shoulder in a sort of knapsack or hobo bundle. And it would not require a Titan to perform this task with a three-year-old in a pillowcase. It would require someone more or less the size of an adult. Someone more or less like a father.

I used to take showers with my dad. I was very little. Around the age when I dreamed of the Giant. I took baths too, but these were under the supervision of my mom. Baths were more elaborate affairs with toys and scary shampoo plunges under a raging faucet. Showers were a different thing. My mom would bring me into the bathroom where my dad awaited me, naked. I do not know if he had already washed himself or if he would do that later. I remember standing between his legs, facing away from him, while he soaped and rinsed me, the water falling from the showerhead far above. Then he would hand me out to my mother, who waited with a large towel. I don't remember when it happened, but at some point these showers with my dad stopped. I took baths, and then I learned to shower by myself. It can't be literally true, but it feels to me that these showers were the last time either of my parents saw my naked body or even touched me in a casual, intimate way.

My dad used to give me rides on his foot. He had silly nicknames for me. And I used to sit on the shut toilet seat and watch him shave. Then all this stopped. By the time I went to school, all these minor daily events had become part of an earlier life. I, Greg the Kindergartener, had a clear sense of a past in which these things had once been but would not come again. Had something happened? Had something changed?

I think my dad had recognized that his son was gay. I did not come out to my parents until I was twenty-seven. Twenty-seven! (And in this context, from the particular angle I am now telling my story, it strikes me that there is something insulting/humiliating in the necessity of coming out to parents who are supposed to have raised you, who are supposed to have known you *intimately* since birth.) Not until I was twenty-seven was it necessary for my parents to think the words. But my father knew. He has said as much since then. He saw that there was something not *normal* about me. That all my friends were girls. That I preferred reading and playing alone to tackle football and wrestling in the mud ponds out in the field behind the subdivision. Once, when I was seven or eight, he attempted an intervention. I was to invite friends from the neighborhood to go for a hike up to Timpanogos Cave. All these friends were to be boys. I knew the boys on the street (although we weren't close pals), and I rounded them up. We went to the cave. It was fine. We came home, and I went back to my life. The real life, the normal life, that seemed neither real nor normal to my dad. But he never tried anything like the field trip again. He just nagged at me that I didn't like to get dirty, I didn't have an instinct for car repair, I was hopeless at casting a fishing line.

I suppose he didn't know how to relate to me. I didn't like the things that he liked. I didn't act the way a boy should. And I think he was afraid of me. Some softness in me stirred his own insecurities. I could never be masculine enough for him, because he could never be man enough to satisfy himself. We both ended up with a potential for love that could not connect. I could not fit myself into the customary forms that male affection allowed: sports, hunting, mechanics. And he could not accept the need that I had for male love. He turned cruel. I withdrew.

Soon enough, in my childhood undergone in suburban, conservative, Mormon Utah, in my American childhood (see above), I could not fully accept my need either. Soon enough, I could not recall why I had longed for the Giant.

Psychologists and therapists engaged in searching for a specifically gay sense of psyche have posited a same-sex version of the old-standby Oedipus complex. I'm not sure how much currency there is left in Oedipus & Family for contemporary psychological thinking. But it is not necessary to load on all the Freudian baggage to imagine that if there *were* such a thing as a gay child (but see above), such a child would have some need to model both gender identity and erotic attraction on a parent or guardian of the matching gender. Of course, any such need, as soon as it poked above the surface, would be brutally attacked and forced back underground, if only to rise again in more fertile fields. The Return of the Return of the Repressed.

Fairy tales (don't think I have lost all sight of Jack here) were the magic beans of my imagined life. One useful thing about the small clutch of tales filling a shelf in most American children's mental libraries is their hollowness. These narratives have gone soft-edged with familiarity, like worn-down board books at a public library. Yet beyond the heavy use, the original purpose, if any, of each tale is obscured, if not absent. Some of these stories can be squeezed for a reductive moral: Little Red Riding Hood's "Don't talk to strangers," for example. And some can be condemned for messages that seem alarming in a contemporary context: Cinderella's suggestion that beauty and tiny feet are the only skill-set a woman needs. Others are hard to parse: What to make of Jack's tale? Go ahead, kids, and trade your cow for beans; they'll help you break-and-enter a castle, steal a golden egg-laying goose, and kill the owner. What lesson should children draw from *that* sequence of events? Bruno Bettelheim and others have proposed a therapeutic use for such stories in aiding children to understand the world and overcome their fears. Those of a Jungian bent might see these tales as part of an imaginal playground; they provide materializations of the archetypes of every child's inner world. In addition to fairy tales' role as moral repository and psychological workout, I would suggest their suitability as an unfettered laboratory for sensual exploration.

Feminists have long worried about a pernicious influence on girls of so many passive storybook heroines who embody virtue in a pretty package of looks and manners—heroines who, if they could be said to possess anything so engaged as a goal, long for home and husband: royal ones. Even Disney—the de facto custodian of cinemized fairy tales—has felt the need to inject its recent heroines with a compensatory syringe full of spunk. Yet I suspect that a survey of the actual fairy princess games of girls would reveal a rather different emphasis. All those skirts and puffed sleeves and conical hats trailing gauze. The real pleasure here may come from swanning and swirling around in silky folds and glittery jewels—even if the gown is a bedsheet or a windbreaker or imaginary. The appeal of marrying a wealthy husband may be more tangential to the experience than the chance to embody the princess in all her sensory splendor.

I never much wanted to be a fairy-tale princess (although many gay boys *do*). I did spend real time in those stories, however. Little Red, and the Three Bears, and Jack and his Beanstalk. I found great appeal in wandering those darkly dangerous forests, roaming inside treasure caves (Open Sesame!), and climbing a vegetable ladder to a grossly oversized castle. And, of course, there was the Giant. Or Paul Bunyan. Or Dad. Or Whoever He Was. Shrugging my way back into boyhood, I can feel that extra prick of interest that encounters with giants always gave me. Jack's. Goldilocks surprised in bed by immense bears. David's Goliath. The Jolly Green Guy. Later, Odysseus and the Cyclops, and the giant that the protagonists encounter in *The Silver Chair* (one of C. S. Lewis's Narnia books). There was a craving there. A need. A quickening. Whatever It Was, it stirred in me.

Fairy tales, and later fantasy books and films and comic books, offered an unregulated sanctuary not only for creatures that could not exist in actuality—talking animals, shoemaking elves, Baba Yaga's chicken-legged house—but for emotions that had no conceivable outlet into reality. I could not be a gay boy in a world where gay boys did not exist, but, then, hobbits, centaurs, and giants had no claim to actuality either yet somehow managed to survive—on the page and in my head if nowhere else. If I could not pursue the Giant in *my* world, Jack could in his.

When, the morning after the fiasco over the cow and his mother's harsh scolding, Jack woke up to the Spectacle of Vegetation outside his window, his first impulse was to climb. It was not to rub his mother's nose in the great green rebuttal to her doubts. Not to grab his scythe and harvest some really really huge bean pods. No, he headed straight for the tallest and sturdiest stalk and started up. This overnight growth was the answer to a preexisting wish. It's phallic, right? You think you're big, Mr. Giant? Well, check out *my* stalk! As much as the beanstalk was Jack's stairway to the stars, an access pass to the Realm of the Giant, it was also Jack's calling card: If you won't come down, look out, I'm coming up.

Given what happened later—Jack's looting of the Giant's larder—it would be logical to conclude that Jack's heart was always set on robbery. Logical but not essential. It is possible that what Jack really wanted from the Giant was recognition. And if he couldn't get affection, he would settle for notoriety.

Jack's Giant, as it turned out, was a monster. Not satisfied with being larger and wealthier than everyone else, he was also—Fee Fi Fo Fum—a cannibal. Rather than wishing to embrace Jack as a father or a lover, he hoped to eat him. To subsume him, to incorporate Jack's flesh and blood into his own gross form. Rather than share his wealth and his knowledge, the Giant hoarded it all. More so, he wanted whatever little scrap Jack could call his own: his independence. Once thoroughly digested, Jack wouldn't be running loose and rebellious with his outrageous ideas about horticulture.

So Jack and the Giant. What a disappointment! Jack with all his expectations, his sensuous edge-of-sleep dreams, had stretched up his stalk, only to meet a hulking beast at the top who denied him everything. Why *not* steal from the jerk? Why *not* abscond with his goose? And when the Giant—alerted by the screeching harp, and full of rage and wounded pride (What is *he* doing here? How could *he* possibly? Who let *him* in?)—came clodding after Jack, why *not* kill the bastard, given the chance? As he took an ax to the bean-stalk, knowing the Giant was in mid-descent, Jack must have sensed that he was finishing off not only the Giant but his dream as well. Unless he chanced on yet another parcel of magic beans, Jack would not be heading back to that castle again, and the Giant, soon to be pulped at the bottom of his own impact crater, would never be a friend to anyone. Jack must have hoped, as he chopped, that those golden eggs would not prove too paltry a consolation.

Jack's later incarnation as the Giant-Killer, his sequel self, is a testament to bad lessons learned. Unable to connect with his own Giant in any fashion besides the murderous, Jack sets out to pro-mote the same solution to others. He becomes a serial killer, ob-sessed with Giants that he can only destroy. The rewards are big, and there's admiration from the menfolk and the adoration of pretty girls. But there's something desperate and smarmy about his enterprise. And these tales of Jack's later exploits make clear that he has become a major creep. His youthful dash and daring, his peasant nose-thumbery, have soured into a mercenary scrounge for a paycheck. He once dreamed of the Giant; now he dreams of the Dollar—and the kingdom lives happily ever after with this change of heart.

But I wonder if Jack . . . the young Jack buried inside the Giant-Killer, who was as unafraid to touch his dangerous desire as he was to touch the string of the traitorous singing harp . . . if this more tender Jack would be happier if he persisted in holding his heart up for a Giant who would not leap to devour it but would wrap Jack's offering with care and carry it next to his own.

Jirí Cêch

BOHEMIAN BEASTS AND THEIR BUTTERY, BUXOM BRIDES

Perhaps my father's strange fairy tales resulted from the peculiar Czechoslovakian darkness and the way those nights smelled. Wild forests of broken brambles and damp moss and pines moaning like women in labor or cows. Not *women in cows*. And not *cows in labor*. Just cows standing in moonlit Moravian pastures mooing because they're dumb.

That's what my cousin Vavrinec says. He's a farmer in what is now the Czech Republic (once Bohemia, now vanished) who really wanted to be an auto mechanic. So maybe he just resents cows for not sounding like an idling V-8 engine. Or maybe cows really are dumb. Not *dumb* as in *mute*. Cows moo, after all. (Q: What do you call a dumb cow? A: Moot.) Though mooing isn't really speaking, is it? A veterinarian would know. Or maybe not. Some vets treat only little nervous dogs with innate psychological disorders that cause them to pee on expensive rugs. The stain on my Aubusson is permanent, says the Afghani rug specialist whose shop is just around the corner from my flat. I invited him up for Turkish coffee one winter afternoon—windows wide open to eliminate the urine odor—so I could elicit his expertise for free. Not that I'm cheap. But it's like this: If you spend only a few dollars on Turkish coffee, plus a painfully boring hour of time chatting about wool and vegetable dyes while dressed in a winter parka, ski cap, and gloves, you can attain a sort of American capitalist nirvana microcosm: *A penny saved is a penny better spent on wine and women.*

Which is, unfortunately, what led to the peeing dog. A woman I briefly dated came home drunk with me (drunk, too) one cheerful night of boozing and blood sucking. I peeled off her tight black leather clothes (oh how she reminded me of the buxom Bulgarian blonde I once chased halfway across Europe just to watch her sway in those leather jeans!), and she peeled off my clothes, though I was wearing a loose silk-blend sweater and gabardine trousers, and we proceeded to have sex. Whereupon her big Balenciaga bag sprang open and out leaped a tiny trembling miniature (!) Chihuahua that, upon witnessing me tangled naked and sweaty with its mistress, went into paroxysms of pissing and whining. The mistress was beside herself. I assuaged her mortification by attempting to pat her little dog on the head. The little bastard bit me. Have you ever noticed how sharp the teeth are on little dogs? They're like . . . like . . . um, the sharp teeth on little fish. At least on little fish that have teeth. I do not think dogfish have teeth. But I could be wrong. I once made a bet with my cousin—not Vavrinec, no, another cousin we used to call Pocení Mazacího Tuku (which means "swelling of grease") because . . . well, I don't really have to explain that one, do I?—bet that some chickens do in fact have teeth, if you consider a cock's comb a real comb, which, as you know, has teeth. But Swelling of Grease proved me wrong by trying to part his hair with a cock's comb. I lost fifty korunas on that one! It was only later I realized that I would have won the bet if the cock had been frozen

solid, which sometimes happens in Bohemian winters. I remember once my father told me about the worst winter ever . . .

Wait.

What was I talking about?

Oh, right—fairy tales.

It appears I have run out of time before reaching my point. Which is: The Czechoslovakian fairy tales my father told me were digressive, pointless exercises in talking for the sake of hearing one's overweening voice. If you were to ask me—though I doubt you ever would because upon meeting me you'd be made mute by my incredible good looks—I would tell you that my father's fairy tales had no influence on me whatsoever.

Alexander Chee

KITSUNE

Most of this story is made of coincidences. Moments that could or could not mean what they could mean.

For example, on a winter afternoon my boyfriend looks up from what he is reading as I am about to run an errand with the car. I am at a cabin in the New Hampshire woods, where I've gone to do some writing, and he is visiting. I have the keys in my hand.

Be careful, he says.

Okay, I say, and as I walk out the door, think on how it is odd. He never says anything of the kind normally. He is the one who is always admonishing me as too careful, always insisting we park illegally or swim without lifeguards. He isn't one to be concerned.

There had been snow recently. I decide to take a dirt road up a steep hill out through the woods, sure that the snow there is still fresh and will hold the wheels of the car. Near the top the car begins to slide backward. The tires won't grip as the new snow fills their grooves and the tires go smooth.

I see something move in the rearview window as the car begins its backward drift, a pale yellow-orange flash through the blue winter dusk. A fox. It has a bit of a grin as it crosses the road, and I look at it a second longer than I might have as I go into the ditch backward.

It is my first time seeing a fox in years. It isn't lost on me that I've seen it in a mirror.

The fox in the myths of Korea, Japan, China, and India is a force of nature, neither good nor evil. It often presents mortals with a test of sincerity to determine whether it awards help or harm. It uses magic to do so.

The fox can change shape and, in the stories that survive to us, has a fondness for taking the forms of lost loves long dead.

In Japan such stories are often called *kitsune,* and this name comes from the name of a farmer who married a beautiful young girl and had a son with her. One day, when she was being chased by a wild dog, she leapt on top of a fence and transformed into a fox. He said to her he still loved her because she had borne him a child. He asked that she come and always sleep with him as she did before she became a fox. *Kitsune* means, "Come to bed."

He gave their son the surname Kitsune. He was said to run as fast as a bird flies. A later descendant, a girl, was reported to be as strong as a hundred men.

In twelfth-century Japan there was a lady of the emperor's court by the name of Lady Tamamo. She became his concubine and was later, as the story goes, revealed to be a fox demon who had assumed the guise of the young woman. In the presence of the court astrologer, a gust of wind blew out all the lamps illuminating the room and she was, to his astonishment, still emitting light. He threatened her life and she revealed her true form, that of a nine-tailed fox.

When a fox reaches the age of a thousand years, she earns her nine tails. The greatest fox of all has one thousand.

Lady Tamamo, or her impersonator, alternately flew away; transformed herself into a stone that emitted, by the force of her evil, poisonous fumes that killed travelers; or was beheaded. In the Kabuki version of this tale, she escapes and transforms into several disguises: a masseur, a man, a courtesan, a god of thunder, a street girl. It seems appropriate for a fox demon who changes shapes to have a story with several endings. All could be true, and she could still be alive.

A story of the stone she left behind comes to us from Bashō, the Japanese pilgrim poet, who visited the stone nearly one hundred years later, found it still emitting poisonous gas, still killing all that came near it, and wrote a poem about the visit. A man in the thirteenth century, sent to purify the Murder Stone, as it became known, had struck it with his staff in his attempt to destroy it, and it split open. He was visited in a dream by the spirit of Lady Tamamo, who told him she wished to be released from her torment by instruction in Buddhism. Her visitor, through a spell, asked for her purification and release. And yet, when Bashō visited the stone, he found it still leaked poison into the air. The legend speaks of the poison as being her hatred and resentment.

She had not, after all, plotted against the emperor's life. She was simply revealed to be a fox among the members of his court.

When I read the story, I had a vision of her in flight, her flame-colored hair behind her in the wind, her silk gown stained with blood, hidden in the clouds, moving across the bay of Japan. There are small islands there, between Korea and Japan, where things get strange. I know this because my family is from those islands, was exiled there when the Chinese empire's control over Korea fell apart more than five hundred years ago. My ancestors were generals and scholars, turned into fishermen. They would understand a disguise, I felt, would understand what it was like to have once been an emperor's favorite and then to be in exile.

I decided to introduce them.

There were many stories of foxes taking the shapes of lost loves to seduce scholars, but always, it seemed, they were women. There were no stories of when the fox took the shape of a lost love who was a man. At the time, I was at work on my first novel, *Edinburgh*, and as soon as I found Tamamo, I knew, my novel was that story, a fox story of when the fox was a man.

I also liked the stories I found about the children of fox demons like Kuzunoha, a fox who leaves when her son discovers she is a fox. He chases her down, and his reward is the gift of being able to speak to any animal. My main character was a character like me but not like me, with a family like mine but not mine. An ancient family with secrets, like her, it seemed to me.

What would have happened, I wondered, if Kuzunoha's son had never discovered the truth, and it went on like that, for generations? And then, what if one day a descendant of his were to figure it out?

And so I had Lady Tamamo land on the beach of an island like the island my family was from, where the water was dark and deep, the island like a submerged mountain. She would wait there for the fishermen to come in, and introduce herself. Perhaps combing her long red hair.

The hair is the one part of the demon that won't transform. It is said to be the way to know a fox when it is in human disguise.

The problem I was trying to solve at the time I discovered the story of Lady Tamamo was that my novel was about sexual abuse and its legacy in adult life, how what happens stays with you and over time you transform into a shell for something angry and full of fear. Something like a Murder Stone. It was, at one point in its life as a manuscript, a difficult novel to read. People told me not to write it. They told me no one would read a novel about teenagers and suicide and sexual abuse. Among the friends who had read it, they told me the first ninety pages were nearly unreadable, for how they were full of pain.

I decided then I needed to make a novel everyone would read about something no one wanted to read about. I wanted people to open it and not stop reading until it was done. There was something I wanted them to know about all this, and it had to be something they would finish.

Think of tests of sincerity.

It was 1998 when I found the foxes. I had a conversation with my friend Shauna Seliy on her porch in Brooklyn, New York, where we were both living at the time. Shauna is a writer and world traveler, the sort of person who has friends in taxis all over New York because of her ability to speak Urdu. At this point I had been writing the novel for over four years, and was just back from a residency at the Virginia Center for the Creative Arts, where I'd written more than a hundred pages in five weeks, almost as much as I'd written in the four previous years. The book had exploded and seemed to be filling out rapidly. I finally knew the plot, the basis of the story: A young man loses his first love, his best friend, to suicide, and blames himself for his friend's death. Both had been sexually molested by their choir director, and he felt his own silence about what had happened to him had doomed his friend to the same experience. Years later he has a teenage student who reminds him of this first love and is, against his will, seduced by him. This student, unbeknownst to him, is the son of his molester, fostered out to his grandparents while his father serves his sentence. The father has just been released from prison and is home again.

I was afraid of the way the book was changing. On the one hand, I wasn't sure of it, and yet, as I put it in place, all of it felt permanent. The plot was something I'd tried to structure after reading Aristotle's *Poetics*. And so what happened next made a great deal of sense.

Somehow, Shauna and I began talking about foxes and her travels in Japan. She was telling me about a visit to a fox shrine. She told me about fox demons, shape changers who take the appearance of lost loves long dead in order to seduce their victims to their death.

I felt something shift. I left Shauna, went to a bookstore where I found, oddly, a compendia of demons. There I found the story of Lady Tamamo.

I remembered being on a boat to my family's island, Narodo, and seeing two little girls in front of me, the sun moving through their hair and the red threads there among the black that seemed so improbable.

Lady Tamamo having left them there, I thought to myself, would make it less improbable.

I went home and began the work of finishing my novel, having come to understand I was writing a fox story.

In retrospect there was a logic to it that made complete sense. I did not make the decision out of logic, however. I made the decision in an instant and the changes were immediate. Now readers read the first ninety pages easily and moved quickly from beginning to end. It was no longer a painful tract, it was now a story about lost love and the shadows at the edges of things.

One thing that foxes can do is possess you.

I remembered a single story of the fox as a child, told to me by my father, now deceased. I remember it involved a fox with a magic ring. I would later wonder if this was the wish-granting jewel of Buddhism, as in the Buddhist vow, be unto others as a wish-granting jewel. The fox is a figure in some of the sects and carries the jewel in its mouth. My father, who told it to me, was not a Buddhist. He was not a Christian. The bank is my church, I remember him telling my mother once. Later, on a visit in Korea, I do recall from my grandfather a sidelong comment I didn't understand, that the fox was the most important animal in Korea.

I don't know why and I didn't ask. On my visits to Korea I felt very much like the wrong sort of grandchild, the lumpen halfbreed who couldn't speak Korean and who couldn't look Korean. How do you tell them apart? a cousin asked me about Americans.

I don't know, I said. I just do.

I didn't tell him the white kids asked me the same question.

Most of my childhood I felt like a shade, something in and out of perception. People would say things about Asian people in front of me that they would never say in front of someone more visibly Asian, and people would say things about white people in front of me that people would never say in front of people more visibly white. I vanished, it felt like. Or my appearance changed. White people thought my eyes were brown and my hair brown. Blacks and Asians thought I had green eyes and red hair. Why would you go to Korea to visit relatives? asked one coworker of mine at a bookstore in San Francisco some years ago.

Because . . . and then I paused in my answer. Because I'm half Korean.

His eyes shot open. No way, he said.

I accepted it then, as a child, in the way children do, that this was what I was, something that changed in the light around people and that I couldn't control or predict. Most people, I think, when they meet other people, are confident that they give the appearance of belonging to this or that ethnic group; they feel confident that there is a home somewhere and a family that looks like them. This was not me, though. My mother was blonde, my father's hair, shoe-polish black. Except for one red hair. Which he would pull out.

My eyes are hazel, half green and half brown. My hair, brown and red.

What was I? It was a question answered every day. I soon realized I could give a different answer every time to the question people always asked me: What are you? It hurt at first, as a child. Why was it no one knew what I was? And why did they seem suspicious, or even resentful? But soon it became a mark of distinction, to be like this. I have been mistaken as Mexican by Mexicans, African American by African Americans, I have been asked by strangers if I am Swedish, Japanese, Chinese, Argentinean, Hawaiian. What was I, indeed. If no one knew, what could I be?

What could I not be?

I have the ordinary strength of a man of my age. I could never run fast. Animals like me but I cannot understand them any better than anyone else. And yet.

In the fall of the year I find the story of Lady Tamamo, I go to Korea and from my grandfather receive a portrait of my deceased grandmother from when she was much younger. Her hair is braided and coiled beautifully to her head. The picture is in black and white. She looks like she has a carefully hidden happiness. Around her neck, a fox. It was an old-fashioned way to make a fox collar, to use the whole skin and fasten the clasp inside the mouth, so that it would look like a fox asleep around your neck, its tail held in its own mouth.

I felt a shock as I took it from him.

I'm sure I'm just being imaginative. I'm sure these are just coincidences.

Robert Coover

TALE, MYTH, WRITER

Tale is the underbelly of myth. Myth is head, tale body; myth power, tale resistance; myth nice, tale naughty; myth structure, tale flow; myth king, tale fool; myth sacred, tale profane; myth father, tale child (though the child, as always, is the father's father); myth tragic, tale comic. Myths are communal dreamlike fantasies (Freud's "daydream of the race"); tales are more about a person's waking life. Where animals talk, magic abounds, and revenge is sweet. Myth lives in bounded places between which wars ensue; tales are, like many of their heroes, homeless wanderers, rarely partisans. "The folktale has no landlord." Whereas myth is meant to introduce the young to the reality principle, tale is said to be a subversive alternative to the official notion of "reality." Yet both are archly conservative, madly wishful, shy of the real. What-if in myth is truth, dogma; in more modest tale, a populist teasing of the imagination. Yet tale is governed by dogma too, a subtler one and more tenacious. Genre is what it's sometimes called. Pattern. The way things are. Myth environs us. Tales do too. They, like the Writer, reside within the Consciousness Industry.

Much of that industry is devoted to sleep and a pampering of the unconscious. Consciousness is an accomplishment which requires enormous effort and so can be maintained only for limited periods, before, with great relief, we sink back into a mindless stupor. Tale has heroic tales about the effort; myth celebrates the stupor. The Consciousness Industry, like any other, survives on profits, and stupor is more profitable than that true consciousness they ostensibly espouse, and so, feeling blameless, they peddle mostly soporifics. The emergence of full consciousness is so rare and difficult, it is often felt as super-natural, sleep (our original Edenic condition) the seductive "natural" state. Odysseus, the adventurous tale hero, resisted the seductive Siren songs of blissful sleep, choosing the pursuit of wakeful consciousness (even so, he had to be lashed to the mast), but most don't. It's too hard, hurts too much. Settle into prime time, go to a movie, watch a game instead. Better not to read at all, certainly nothing by the Writer. Who . . .

As the story goes, Tale, once-uponing, sallies forth on the next and next adventure; Myth (same family) stays at home and rules the roost. The Writer, Tale-like, sallies forth as well and, as though a character in Tale's own tale, bumps into Tale upon the road. Sometimes they fight. Sometimes they carouse and drink together. The Writer is always wary, though, for Tale is a tricky bastard without scruples who can catch you from behind and steal your wit without your even knowing it. That's bad, but can be worse when Myth's the foe. To be chicaned by Tale, the Writer knows, is not the same as falling into Myth's iron clutches. Tale will often laugh and let you go; Myth's fiercer, humorless, unyielding. Tale sends you down the open road (even if it's always the same road); Myth's mansion, for all its inviting intricacy of well-appointed rooms and corridors, has drawn curtains and locked doors and attic horrors one cannot always avoid.

The Writer, house-breaker by profession, intrudes brazenly upon Myth's mansion, at the risk of getting lost and never coming out again, and at the greater risk of finding comfort in it, as so many do, and forgetting the reasons for breaking in. Which are: to do a bit of creative redecorating, let the light in, turn the statuary back to flesh again, stake revenant hearts with jokes, yes, but more than that: (Its foundations are imaginary! The Writer knows this!) to bring the whole house down if possible. Thus, the Writer, too, madly wishful, avoids the real. Such are the self-delusions necessary for all romantic quests; this no exception. For Myth's no pushover, has been in the neighborhood as long as memory; the

Writer's days, contrarily, are precious few. You just get started and . . .

One surprise: Tale's here, Myth's unreliable servant, guests' sometime guide, providing relief from tedium and occasional glimpses of the floor plan. Myth is master of this domain and Tale is much constrained, unsmiling, out of rags and into uniform, unvoiced by the master's insistence upon proprieties but able still on the sly to lift carpets or floorboards to reveal the buried remnants of the original humble outdoor stage or to blight the grandeur of a room with a gassy burp or the subtle stubbing of a toe. Tale also, with quiet nods, points out the exits, useful even when (a trickster, Tale) they're trompe l'oeils only. If nothing else, Tale, touring targets, keeps the Writer in motion. Keep moving, that's what Odysseus said. Stop your ears and keep moving.

The Writer, from time to time, when weary of these airless exploits, escapes to mix again with the hoi polloi and breathe the common air and, looking back, sees that Myth's mansion, for all the Writer's heroic depredations, is still as imposing as ever, seemingly unchanged. Hmm. Does it tilt just a little to the left now? Is that a broken window? No, probably just the way the shadows fall. Along comes raggedy Tale again, and they have a friendly tussle, just for old times' sake, and while Tale has the Writer pinned, and in response to the Writer's disheartened mien, tells stories of heroes who, against insuperable odds, defeated giants, beheaded dragons, won princesses and kingdoms. In each of these stories, the Writer knows, the hero was defeated, but the story doesn't say so, the moral being: you are a clown, this is what you do, take your falls, get up again to take another. Tale also tells the story of the minstrel whose only listeners were animals who simply wished to eat him but were stayed by the minstrel's music; eventually, of course, when the minstrel ran out of fresh tunes, they did eat him, but meanwhile . . .

The Consciousness Industry maintains Myth's mansion very well, repairs the road Tale travels on, and tolerates the Writer when it is convenient to do so, preferring marginalization to the gallows (not always), well aware that the Writer's bad behavior will be industrial fodder a generation on, the stuff of T-shirts and classrooms and bitter laments about the very industry that profits from them. Thus the Writer's heroics, for all their grand ambitions, go largely unnoticed in their time, come to little. Except for irony. It is the gift of irony, denied Myth and mostly over Tale's head, that is the Writer's portion.

Neil Gaiman

FOUR POEMS

I don't honestly know what I think about fairy tales, because they are part of me. It would be like trying to explain what I think of my spine or my circulatory system or my eyes. The tales I read as a boy define how I see the world and how I perceive what I see; they flow through me, and, sometimes still, they hold me up. I write stories as an adult in which the membrane of the world is thin and permeable and in which something more real exists beneath and above, and, truly, that is the world I believe in. (Do I mean that literally? Certainly, although *literal* means constructed of words, and it is stories, constructed of words, that we are discussing here.) The road between dreams and reality is one that must be negotiated, not walked.

I decided, on reflection, that rather than making an ass of myself writing about fairy tales, it would be far more sensible to write about four poems. These are poems I have written, over the years, about what I believe about fairy tales. One poem is about making stories up, one is about passing stories on, one about surviving stories and the use of stories for survival, and one is about what we get to take away, at the end.

This is the first: a poem once called, simply, "Instructions." I wanted it to be, when I wrote it, a set of instructions for navigating and surviving a fairy tale, but now, looking it over, I wonder if it is not also about being young and having choices.

Instructions

Touch the wooden gate in the wall you never saw before
Say "please" before you open the latch,
go through,
walk down the path.
A red metal imp hangs from the green-painted front door,
as a knocker,
do not touch it; it will bite your fingers.
Walk through the house. Take nothing. Eat nothing.
However,
if any creature tells you that it hungers,
feed it.
If it tells you that it is dirty,
clean it.
If it cries to you that it hurts,
if you can,
ease its pain.

From the back garden you will be able to see the wild wood.
The deep well you walk past leads down to Winter's realm;
there is another land at the bottom of it.
If you turn around here,
you can walk back, safely;
you will lose no face. I will think no less of you.

Once through the garden you will be in the wood.
The trees are old. Eyes peer from the undergrowth.
Beneath a twisted oak sits an old woman. She may ask for something;
give it to her. She
will point the way to the castle. Inside it
are three princesses.
Do not trust the youngest. Walk on.
In the clearing beyond the castle the twelve months sit about a fire,
warming their feet, exchanging tales.
They may do favours for you, if you are polite.
You may pick strawberries in December's frost.

Trust the wolves, but do not tell them where you are going.
The river can be crossed by the ferry. The ferryman will take you.
(The answer to his question is this:
If he hands the oar to his passenger, he will be free to leave the boat.
Only tell him this from a safe distance.)

If an eagle gives you a feather, keep it safe.
Remember: that giants sleep too soundly; that
witches are often betrayed by their appetites;
dragons have one soft spot, somewhere, always;
hearts can be well hidden,
and you betray them with your tongue.

Do not be jealous of your sister:
know that diamonds and roses
are as uncomfortable when they tumble from one's lips as toads and
frogs:
colder, too, and sharper, and they cut.

Remember your name.
Do not lose hope—what you seek will be found.
Trust ghosts. Trust those that you have helped to help you in their
turn.
Trust dreams.
Trust your heart, and trust your story.

When you come back, return the way you came.
Favours will be returned, debts be repaid.
Do not forget your manners.
Do not look back.
Ride the wise eagle (you shall not fall)
Ride the silver fish (you will not drown)
Ride the grey wolf (hold tightly to his fur).

There is a worm at the heart of the tower; that is why it will not stand.

When you reach the little house, the place your journey started,
you will recognise it, although it will seem much smaller than you
remember.
Walk up the path, and through the garden gate you never saw before
but once.
And then go home. Or make a home.

Or rest.

Of course, fairy tales are transmissible. You can catch them, or be
infected by them. They are the currency that we share with those
who walked the world before ever we were here. (Telling stories to
my children that I was, in my turn, told by my parents and grandparents makes me feel part of something special and odd, part of
the continuous stream of life itself.) My daughter Maddy is now
eleven, and we still share stories, but they are now on television
or from films. We read the same books and talk about them, but I
no longer read them to her, and even that was a poor replacement
for telling stories out of my head.

I believe we owe it to each other to tell stories. It's as close to a
credo as I have or will, I suspect, ever get.

Locks
We owe it to each other to tell stories,
as people simply, not as father and daughter.
I tell it to you for the hundredth time:

*"There was a little girl, called Goldilocks,
for her hair was long and golden,
and she was walking in the Wood and she saw—"*

"—cows." You say it with certainty,
remembering the strayed heifers we saw in the woods
behind the house, last month.

*"Well, yes, perhaps she saw cows,
but also she saw a house."*

"—a great big house," you tell me.
"No, a little house, all painted, neat and tidy."

"A great big house."
You have the conviction of all two-year-olds.
I wish I had such certitude.

"Ah. Yes. A great big house.
And she went in . . ."

I remember, as I tell it, that the locks
of Southey's heroine had silvered with age.
The Old Woman and the Three Bears . . .
Perhaps they had been golden once, when she was a child.

And now, we are already up to the porridge,
"And it was too—"
"—hot!"
"And it was too—"
"—cold!"
And then it was, we chorus, *"just right."*

The porridge is eaten, the baby's chair is shattered,
Goldilocks goes upstairs, examines beds, and sleeps,
unwisely.

But then the bears return.
Remembering Southey still, I do the voices:
Father Bear's gruff boom scares you, and you delight in it.

When I was a small child and heard the tale,
if I was anyone I was Baby Bear,
my porridge eaten, and my chair destroyed,
my bed inhabited by some strange girl.

You giggle when I do the baby's wail,
"Someone's been eating my porridge, and they've eaten it—"

"All up," you say. A response it is,
Or an amen.

The bears go upstairs hesitantly,
their house now feels desecrated. They realise
what locks are for. They reach the bedroom.
"Someone's been sleeping in my bed."
And here I hesitate, echoes of old jokes,
soft-core cartoons, crude headlines, in my head.

One day your mouth will curl at that line.
A loss of interest, later, innocence.
Innocence, as if it were a commodity.
"And if I could," my father wrote to me,
huge as a bear himself, when I was younger,
"I would dower you with experience, without experience."
And I, in my turn, would pass that on to you.
But we make our own mistakes. We sleep
unwisely.
It is our right. It is our madness and our glory.
The repetition echoes down the years.
When your children grow; when your dark locks begin to silver,
when you are an old woman, alone with your three bears,
what will you see? What stories will you tell?

*"And then Goldilocks jumped out of the window
and she ran—"*
Together, now: *"All the way home."*

And then you say, *"Again. Again. Again."*

We owe it to each other to tell stories.

These days my sympathy's with Father Bear.
Before I leave my house I lock the door,
and check each bed and chair on my return.

Again.

Again.

Again.

One thing that puzzles me (and I use *puzzle* here in the technical Humpty Dumpty sense of *really, really irritates me*) is reading, as from time to time I have, learned academic books on folktales and fairy stories that explain why nobody wrote them and go on to point out that looking for authorship of folktales is in itself a fallacy, the kind of books or articles that give the impression that all stories were stumbled upon or reshaped, and I think "Yes, but they all started somewhere, in someone's head." Because stories start in minds—they aren't artifacts or natural phenomena.

One scholarly book I read explained that any fairy story in which a character falls asleep obviously began life as a dream, that was recounted on waking by a primitive type unable to tell dreams from reality, and this was the starting point for our fairy stories, a theory which seemed filled with holes from the get-go, because stories, the kind that survive and are retold, have narrative logic, not dream logic.

Stories are made up by people who make them up. If they work, they get retold. There's the magic of it.

Scheherazade as a narrator was a fiction, as was her sister and the murderous king they needed nightly to placate. The *Arabian Nights* themselves are a fictional construct, assembled from a variety of places, and Aladdin himself is a late tale, folded into the *Nights* by the French only a few hundred years ago. Which is another way of saying that when it began, it certainly didn't begin as I describe. And yet. And still.

Inventing Aladdin
In bed with him that night, like every night,
her sister at their feet, she ends her tale,
then waits. Her sister quickly takes her cue,

and says, "I cannot sleep. Another, please?"
Scheherazade takes one small nervous breath
and she begins, "In faraway Peking
there lived a lazy youth with his mama.
His name? Aladdin. His papa was dead . . . "
She tells them how a dark magician came,
claiming to be his uncle, with a plan.
He took the boy out to a lonely place,
Gave him a ring he said would keep him safe,
down to a cavern filled with precious stones,
"Bring me the lamp!" and when Aladdin does,
In darkness he's abandoned and entombed . . .

There now.
          Aladdin locked beneath the earth,
she stops, her husband hooked for one more night.

Next day
she cooks
she feeds her kids
she dreams . . .
Knowing Aladdin's trapped,
and that her tale
has bought her just one day.
What happens now?
She wishes that she knew.

It's only when that evening comes around
and husband says, just as he always says,
"Tomorrow morning, I shall have your head"
when Dunyazade, her sister, asks, "But please,
what of Aladdin?" only then, she knows . . .

And in a cavern hung about with jewels
Aladdin rubs his lamp. The Genie comes.
The story tumbles on. Aladdin gets

the princess and a palace made of pearls.
Watch now, the dark magician's coming back:
"New lamps for old," he's singing in the street.
Just when Aladdin has lost everything,
she stops.
        He'll let her live another night.

Her sister and her husband fall asleep.
She lies awake and stares up in the dark
Playing the variations in her mind:
the ways to give Aladdin back his world
His palace, his princess, his everything.
And then she sleeps. The tale will need an end,
but now it melts to dreams inside her head.

She wakes,
She feeds the kids
She combs her hair
She goes down to the market
Buys some oil
The oil-seller pours it out for her,
decanting it
from an enormous jar.
She thinks,
What if you hid a man in there?
She buys some sesame as well, that day.

Her sister says, "He hasn't killed you yet."
"Not yet." Unspoken waits the phrase, "He will."

In bed she tells them of the magic ring
Aladdin rubs. Slave of the Ring appears . . .
Magician dead, Aladdin saved, she stops.
But once the story's done, the teller's dead,
her only hope's to start another tale.
Scheherazade inspects her store of words,

half-built, half-baked ideas and dreams combine
with jars just big enough to hide a man,
And she thinks, Open Sesame, and smiles.
"Now, Ali Baba was a righteous man,
but he was poor . . ." she starts, and she's away,
and so her life is safe for one more night,
until she bores him, or invention fails.

She does not know where any tale waits
before it's told. (No more do I.)
But forty thieves sounds good, so forty
thieves it is. She prays she's bought another clutch of days.

We save our lives in such unlikely ways.

This one started with pondering what it is we want in a fairy story,
what it is we set out after, and what it is we get. And then wondering why there were very few elderly heroes in fairy tales and
deciding that it's because they've already had their stories. That after the happily-ever-after comes, or doesn't, that's where we get
our villains from, not to mention our wizards, our wise-women
who will offer advice in exchange for a little of your bread and
cheese. They had their stories when they were young. And now
they have someone else's.

Boys and Girls Together
Boys don't want to be princes.
Boys want to be shepherds who slay dragons,
maybe someone gives you half a kingdom and a princess,
but that's just what comes of being a shepherd boy
and slaying a dragon. Or a giant. And you don't really
even have to be a shepherd. Just not a prince.

In stories, even princes don't want to be princes,
disguising themselves as beggars or as shepherd boys,
leaving the kingdom for another kingdom,

princehood only of use once the ogre's dead, the tasks are
    done,
and the reluctant king, her father, needing to be convinced.

Boys do not dream of princesses who will come for them.
Boys would prefer not to be princes,
and many boys would happily kiss the village girls,
out on the sheep-moors, of an evening,
over the princess, if she didn't come with the territory.

Princesses sometimes disguise themselves as well,
to escape the kings' advances, make themselves ugly,
soot and cinders and donkey girls,
with only their dead mothers' ghosts to aid them,
a voice from a dried tree or from a pumpkin patch.
And then they undisguise, when their time is upon them,
gleam and shine in all their finery. Being princesses.
Girls are secretly princesses.

None of them know that one day, in their turn,
Boys and girls will find themselves become
bad kings or wicked stepmothers,
aged woodcutters, ancient shepherds, mad crones and
    wise-women,
to stand in shadows, see with cunning eyes:
The girl, still waiting calmly for her prince.
The boy, lost in the night, out on the moors.

Johannes Göransson

MUTILATED ANIMALS
Folktales and Modern Swedish Poetry

I.

I grew up in Skåne, the southernmost province of Sweden, consisting mainly of farmland. In many of the fields there are burial mounds from the Bronze Age (ten to fifteen feet tall). My grade-school class used to go to play at one of these mounds in a field just outside Håstad, the small town where the school was located. This particular mound was unusual: there was a large gash in the side of it. The farmer who owned the field had tried to get rid of the mound in order to make his farming more efficient. However, he got in only one day's work. For that night he was awakened by a terrible din. When he ran outside, he saw that his animal barn was on fire. The clamor of his horses' and pigs' screaming and trying to break out of the burning barn shocked his entire body. Ever since he had been paralyzed on one side of his body and half blind.

The farmer was married to my grade-school teacher, a kindly but stern and devout lady. I would see him around town dragging his bad leg. He had an intriguingly pathetic air about him in his filthy overalls and wrinkled face. Perhaps this makes it a folktale instead of a fairy tale. Perhaps it makes it gossip. In Sweden they just referred to such stories as *sagor*, or tales, but this is not the kind of tale you will find in any anthology. There is no official version, no original text. For all I know, I may have made it up myself. I am one of a very limited number of people to know about it (there can't be more than a hundred people living in Håstad, and certainly the farmer and his devout wife are both dead by now).

However, the story is by no means unique. The style and the theme are recognizable from other, more official tales. There is, for example, the story of Odin's Eye, a perfectly round, bottomless lake in Skåne. According to the old Viking myth, Odin threw an eye into a well and this allowed him to see the future. But that's not the tale I'm thinking of. The one I'm thinking of I was told as a child: As modern civilization was taking over the country, measuring and explaining with scientific method, the magical creatures who used to inhabit the countryside fled down into the bottomless lake. When scientists heard about the lake, they were naturally curious to measure its depth, since there is no such thing as a bottomless lake. They brought their measuring device and lowered it down in the water. They kept lowering and lowering it down but it never seemed to reach a bottom. Finally it caught. But when they pulled up the instrument, they did not find soil in the instrument. Rather, the skeleton of a whole bull was clamped to it. This was a sign for the scientists and, by implication, all modern people, to stay away from the lake. The trolls and fairies might have given up the world, but they were still dangerous, threatening.

In both stories, there is a conflict between modern society and the old superstitions. The modern world has more or less taken over the world, but the old superstitions are not to be disrespected. They allegorize the intersection of modernity and superstition, but the kind of knowledge that comes out of the stories is not explanatory in the way natural science, sociology, or even literary interpretations are explanatory; they are explanatory as obfuscation, anti-explanation.

What interests me most of all with both stories is the violent, allegorical-seeming imagery of the story. Why is the barn burned down, rather than the house? Why is the farmer struck blind (as opposed to killed)? Why the cattle skeleton? In myths the logic of such details is available to the audience. These stories use the vehicle of code but without the tenor. The morals are obvious and simplistic in both stories, but the visual imagery overwhelms the morals.

Following the lead of the German Romantics, Samuel Taylor Coleridge famously defined the "symbol" as superior to "allegory." Coleridge opposed the allegory as "a translation of abstract notions into a picture language, which is nothing but an abstraction from the objects of the senses." He opposed this "counterfeit" rhetorical tool with the symbol, which "partakes of the reality which it renders intelligible; and while it enunciates the whole, abides itself as a living part of the unity of which it is representative." Coleridge felt that the symbol organically explained itself, while the allegory was artificial in that you needed a key to unlock its riddle.

These *sagor* resemble the allegory in that they do not explain themselves. However, the key has been thrown away. I find the lack of code liberating: unable to transform the images into meaning, I can revel in the ruins. So much critical work on stories focuses on how to interpret them, as if the interpretation is a way of solving a problem, a way for a culture uncomfortable with the unknown. Even "realism" has to be interpreted as mimesis. The tales let things remain intensively strange.

2.

I may have given you a sort of primitivizing image of Sweden, an image of a legendary land of peasants who set out oatmeal to keep the gnomes happy. But I grew up in a very modern country. We had televisions (and even videos) and movie theaters playing Hollywood blockbusters. We had immigrants (my best friend's dad, Renzo, had come from Italy). We did not have any poverty or homelessness. We had a very progressive education system and a 99 percent literacy rate. Most of the people of Håstad took the train into the city (Lund) every morning to work in offices and factories. Very few people were still farmers. And yet the superstitious world of the old stories remained intertwined in this ultramodernity.

One strain of contemporary Swedish poetry makes use of this

folktale imagination without being sentimental about it. Poets like Aase Berg (b. 1967) and Ann Jäderlund (b. 1951) invoke the violent, allegorical-seeming language and menacing strangeness to derail interpretations and promote a kind of antisymbolic reading style.

Jäderlund stirred up a big debate in 1989 and 1990 when she released the books *Som En Gång Varit Äng* (*Which Once Was Meadow*) and *Snart Går Jag i Sommaren Ut* (*Soon into the Summer I Will Walk Out*). Critics expressed bewilderment at the poems. But the problem was not the conventional difficulty of high modernist abstruseness or allusiveness (any such high modernist qualities would have made it easier for the critics). The poems are very concrete, but something is lacking: What is the point of these poems? What do they communicate? This initial critique was followed by a feminist critique of the male critics, suggesting the male critics were unable to grasp Jäderlund's poetry because it was *écriture féminine*. This controversy marked the beginning of a whole new generation of women writers—including Berg—who started publishing in the 1990s.

At this point I would like to look at a specific part from *Soon into the Summer I Will Walk Out* to figure out just what is so difficult about these poems:

The big valley is a vast mother-of-pearl mirror. There walks the large dead swan in her dead shroud. And there walk the mother-of-pearl children. Or the fragile foundling clumps. That grow out of the virgin mother's throat. They led the swan into a forest and placed beautiful white stones of mother-of-pearl on her back. *Go now and eat that which you have taken from the swans.* Then one ran up and cut a branch from the tree and grabbed a *burning branch* and stuck it into her throat. And scrubbed her both up top and down below. Until the swan's flesh fell off in beautiful heavy clumps. For some time the swan lay in the bushes and slept. And black merchants came riding on black mother-of-pearl horses. Then they took the swan and carried her away.[1]

1. Ann Jäderlund, *Dikter 1984–2000* (Stockholm: Månpocket, 2002), 206, my translation.

The full sequence is fifteen sections long, but this poem offers a good example of this sequence as a whole: the awkward, simple, ungrammatical sentences; the somewhat erratic use of italics; the concrete imagery; the extreme violence depicted without alarm; the attention to the natural world; and, perhaps most important, the mysteriousness of the events.

Most critics have recognized that the poems evoke historical allegories, but they did not point out that the poems are in fact a kind of translation or collage of a specific medieval Swedish text—*Själens Tröst* (The Soul's Consolation)—a religious document "written" at Vadstena Cloister in 1420. Jäderlund uses this text as a source text to create a collage of various sentences; she translates lines from the medieval Swedish of the original text and changes the content slightly. As Jäderlund herself describes her method in an e-mail to me:

> I have straight-up picked out certain sentences. For example, "They took the swan and carried her away." But in the original it's a mule, which is stolen from a lion who is supposed to guard the mule for the Holy Hieronymus and his monastery. The lion gets scared when "black merchants" come to steal the mule, and as a result is forced to do the labor of the mule: carry wood on its back. In the end the lion decides to steal back the mule, as well as all the merchants' riches. But Hieronymus forgives them and gives them back their riches. The conclusion is that one should treat one's fellow Christian with respect.

It is from *Själens Tröst* that Jäderlund derives both the allegorical style and the awkward diction that characterize her style.

The original critics' main problem with this text is that we are not given enough of a framework so that we can unlock what appears to be an allegory. The allegories and parables from *Själens Tröst* end with the wise narrator explaining the symbolic meaning of the (often weird and violent) stories in terms of Christian dogma. That is a part that Jäderlund leaves out; she leads the reader to read the text as allegory through her mysterious specificity of imagery but does not supply a crib sheet. The causality remains hidden. We know that the swan is not just a swan: She has a "shroud" and "walks," for example. She also appears to be more than just a code word for a human being because she can walk despite being "dead"; after her flesh is peeled off, the black merchants can still carry her away. The swan must mean something else, but we don't know what. If the "swan" is not a mere swan, perhaps "children" are not children, "dead" may not even mean dead. Language is destabilized. Jäderlund finds a strange fairy tale inside the authoritative, controlling dogma of Christianity.

In her use of allegory, Jäderlund follows the example of Walter Benjamin, who preferred the obvious artificiality of baroque allegory to the false organic-ness of the symbol. By removing the interpretative frame to the allegory, she creates an experience that is neither symbolic nor naturalistic; it is an intense experience of artificiality. While symbol has traditionally been seen as more egalitarian than allegorical, Jäderlund shows how the use of allegory can be liberating. She writes in an e-mail to me:

> I experienced the allegory as less colonializing, that it did not have the hierarchy, that it was more egalitarian [than "the symbol"]. I think the development goes parallel to the development of religion, from more concrete to more abstract, and I prefer the more concrete, I see it as less dominating . . . less defining, that there is more freedom.

What Coleridge saw as an advantage of the symbol—that it contained its own directions for explication—is "colonializing" to Jäderlund. What Coleridge saw as "organic," she sees as "dominating" and prescriptive.

3.

Aase Berg has taken the flat, allegorical style of *sagor* and applied it to varying aspects of the modern world. In her first collection, *Hos Rådjur* (*With Deer*), Berg brings the threatening world of the folktales into the modern world of suburbs and horror movies, finding the menacing strangeness inside the modern world, which claims to have eradicated superstition. For example, in the poem "I Marsvins Grottan" ("In the Guinea Pig Cave," from *Remainland: Selected Poems of Aase Berg*) the threat of the trolls has been channeled into the very suburban pet, the guinea pig:

> There lay the guinea pigs. There lay the guinea pigs and waited with blood around their mouths like my sister. There lay the guinea pigs and smelled bad in the cave. There lay my sister and swelled and ached and throbbed. There lay the guinea pigs and ached all over and their legs stuck straight up like beetles.

We are no longer out in the fields but in the suburbs. The animals are no longer horses or pigs but pet guinea pigs. And yet we are still in the fairy-tale imagination in the way the animals are both codelike and absolutely literal in their violence. In this way they also connect horror movies to the folktales.

Berg's poems set words in circulation much like an allegory sets emblems into circulation. It doesn't work to read them in the symbolist mode. Instead they assume the artificiality of the allegory. To quote Gilles Deleuze and Félix Guattari's study of that other fairy-talist, Kafka, we can say that Berg

> kills all metaphor, all symbolism, all signification, no less than all designation. Metamorphosis is the contrary of metaphor. There is no longer any proper sense or figurative sense, but only a distribution of states that is part of the range of the word.[2]

We cannot read the guinea pigs as symbols, and yet we cannot solve their presence in the text as mimesis either. They remain strange and violent.

In her massive, hallucinatory second book, *Mörk Materia* (*Dark Matter*), the fairy-tale world moves out of the private sexual discomforts of suburbia and takes on the threatening outside world,

---

2. Gilles Deleuze and Félix Guattari, *Kafka: Toward a Minor Literature,* trans. Dana Polin (Minneapolis: University of Minnesota Press, 1986), 22.

the world people in Sweden may watch with horror on television. The book depicts a postcataclysmic world of environmental catastrophes, genocide, and drug-induced paranoia. We walk into "Bosnia of Graves" and other horrific landscapes (from "4.4 The Animal Gap" in *Remainland*):

> We moved through the body toward a hard environment of large pipes in knots capitals. They rose stoutly toward the fire-blue sky of refineries. There a cloud waited to be released from skin. I would like you Ivo to receive my teeth, my extricated enamels here in the box pulled out of my jaw. My mouth is large and soft with flesh; the material of which animals are made.

In this passage the violent imagery moves both out into the world of newscasts and into the body itself. Science and industry are pulled into the text, while teeth are pulled out of the speaker's mouth. The inside body and the outside world merge in one violent tale.

The ultimate effect of this in-and-out movement is a kind of vertigo. In her book on postmodern Swedish women poets, *Jag själv ett hus av ljus* (*I Myself a House of Light*), Åsa Beckman writes about reading Berg's work:

> When I read her work I notice how my consciousness tries to separate, categorize and make sense of her almost hallucinatory images, but they keep collapsing over and over. I get nauseous, almost seasick from her texts. It is as if there was no sorting authoritative *I* in the poems.[3]

This flat, characterless aesthetic has much in common with the world of the burning barn. If there is a moral to the book, it's that humans have ruined the world. But as with the burning barn, this idea is overwhelmed by the violent imagery. There is no "signification" to help us through the massive heap of images, only "a distribution of states."

3. Åsa Beckman, *Jag själv ett hus av ljus—10 kvinnliga poeter* (Stockholm: Albert Bonniers Förland, 2002), 116, my translation.

In her third book, *Forsla Fett (Transfer Fat)*, Berg plays with the arbitrariness of allegorical language, applying it to the female body and pregnancy and turning the body into a grotesque mystery. Science may claim to have naturalized such weird events as pregnancy and birth, but even science has its fairy tales. Much of the stringy, reverberating language of the book is based on Berg's translation of scientific tracts on string theory written in English:

> *The Hare Infects Dad with Rabies*
> Hare-spring conduit
> hare track
> rabies is freedom
> in the year of the Hare
>
> Here in the black fathermilk
> of loneliness
> from the man in the woods
> with hare[4]

Through her punning Berg intertwines anatomy and the old tale-diction: here mysteries are not relegated to a lake, but to the regions of the human body.

In her most recent book, *Uppland*, the syllables of language themselves take on an animistic energy, setting a fairy-tale ecology in motion around the listless "I" of a plane crash victim, who is also a mother whose family lives an idyllic but isolated life. The book is based on a plane crash that took place in the province of Uppland in 1991, an event that the news media immediately turned into a symbol of the demise of the social welfare state. Berg enters this overtly symbolic event with her fairy-tale diction, imbuing the overdramatic news media:

> *Foot Buoy*
> Hold on to one's skin
> fasten the wing skin

4. Berg, *Remainland*, 49.

Dragon phase unfolds
in a standstilldance
earthbalance[5]

The plane never fully lands but remains in a *"stillståndsdans"*
("standstilldance") that cannot be reduced to the simplistic morality of media symbolism or even the simple language of newspa-
perspeak. It is a dance that is at once technological and ancient.

4.

I may have made up the story about the burning barn as a child.
But if I did, I only used tools that had been given to me. The ratio-
nal modern state has not been able to eradicate these tools and
may, in the end, as Berg suggests, merely be an invention of such
tools—the social welfare state as a myth of sanity and safety. Whatever their agency, the tales persist. They mark the slash in the burial mound, the seam in the earth, the site where the private sick-
ness of the lame farmer comes out to meet the rural child's public
gaze. The state cannot provide a code, cannot stop the meanings
from reverberating.

5. Berg, *Remainland,* 91.

Ilya Kaminsky

THE LITTLE POT

A slender girl and her mother lived in our town, good people but poor. They had nothing to eat, like everyone else in our town.

The girl was always wandering in the forest. She walked, snapping the branches, scaring the squirrels, looking for something to put in her mouth. Here the page turns.

Looking for something to put in her mouth, the slender girl met an old crone.

The old crone did not live in this story; she was only a visitor. Because she was only a visitor, she could not hear but only see the unspoken words each hungry girl, opening her mouth, makes.

The crone didn't hear a word, but her hand stretched out and opened. And in the open hand was a pot.

A little pot. From nothing, it appeared.

The crone said: "When you are hungry, say, 'Cook, little pot, cook,' and the pot will give you sweet porridge." And she said a few other words.

The old crone smiled and vanished from this tale.

As for the slender girl, she did what girls do when given something to keep: she ran home to tell her mother. And they whispered, "Cook, little pot, cook," as they ate sweet porridge. And they ate.

And the pot cooked and they kept whispering, and the pot kept cooking, and the porridge was good.

The pages keep turning. Here, they feed another hungry child. Here, they share their food. Here, the mother kisses the girl lightly. The girl walks to school where she learns from books about other books. And her mother whispers, "Cook, little pot, cook."

The pot cooked as the mother ate, the pot cooked. The mother ate and became full and asked the pot to stop—but she forgot the words to make it stop. Her slender girl knew the words, but she was at school and so the pot kept cooking. And so the mother kept eating. And the porridge kept bubbling over the top.

And it cooked onto the next page and the next. And the kitchen floor was soon covered with porridge, and the tables covered with porridge and the chairs. Then the stove covered, and then the bedroom. And the pot did what pots do, so the porridge began to drip on the sidewalks, on the staircases. The next house was covered with sweet porridge, the nearby street covered: its barbershop and its tailor shop and its bakery. And the neighbors sat on the pavement, eating. The porridge was sweet. And it rose to the branches, and the birds landed and swam and washed themselves. And they ate. And dogs swam and ate. And the chickens made tiny noises. And then they began to drown.

Everyone prayed for the pot to stop cooking, and everyone ate.
Everyone ate and choked and wanted to stop and choked.
No one could stop.
At last—for there's always "at last" in the fairy tale—only one house remained that was not covered with sweet porridge to its copper roof. All the neighbors sat on that roof and ate, their feet dangling in porridge.
At last.
The girl returned from school with two large books.
She said, "Stop, little pot, stop."
The little pot stopped cooking.
The townspeople all looked at one another and shook their heads. In their dark hair shook small pieces of dried porridge.

This is how I remember my childhood. First a fantasia of plenty, yes, but then eating my way back through time.

The second tale begins: Eighteen-year-old peasant girl Natalia and her husband, a white army officer, had a baby girl, six months old.

They walked the streets of Odessa with a cradle and ate chocolate cakes at Deribasovskaya. He bought her an umbrella and she was learning French. In the seventh month the government changed. The white army officer had to escape because the color of his uniform was politically incorrect. Or perhaps something else about him was incorrect, political or not; in any case, he escaped from this story. But Natalia stayed; her baby girl was seven months old.

In the eighth month the government closed the borders. Natalia began to sew so she could buy food. She sewed day and night for the opera singers, she walked behind the stage after the performance, taking measurements, giving compliments, taking measurements; they loved her. Natalia was sewing, the opera was singing, the soup was in the little pot, the baby was turning nine months old.

In the tenth month the government prevented the food from coming into our province. It was an easy month. The opera was still open, the audiences still arrived. But soon the audiences began to walk out of the cities. They thought they could find food in the neighboring villages. But there was no food in the neighboring villages, there was no food in the farthest villages either, but they did not learn of that; they died midway. And the borders remained closed. And there was no food on the table, there was no table, and there was no food even in the little pot. And the bellies began to sing, and then they stopped.

And the baby began its eleventh month. The opera singers left. Natalia did not leave. Natalia ate the earth. She buried her baby girl, she put her into the box from the sewing machine and dug the hole herself. She did everything herself. She even survived on her own somehow. She even married somehow. She even managed not to have another child—holding out till she was forty years old. Even that she did herself, against her new husband's wishes. When she was forty, everything changed. Everything changed. She adopted my father. Everything changed. She told him the story when she taught him how to cook, how to chop vegetables, how to pinch the spices into the little pot. Her finger would weave through the air as she spoke. It landed on his forehead. "You must remember this."

There was once a man who lived in an empire preoccupied with food. It was said of him that he opened an underground business that sold soups so good that when government officials tasted them, their eyes lit up, and they carried that light into the higher offices and courts but could no longer pretend to be loyal to the system that ruled us—and they all lost their offices. But the soup factory kept going, tomato soups and spinach soups and onion soups with fish. His name was Vitya. He was of middle height, and at the time of my birth, his second son, he was middle-aged.

Tomato soup was not merely of a physical world—not as far as my father was concerned. What we put in our mouths feeds not only our bodies but also what lives inside our bodies. There was something strange about that illegal soup factory on Sovetskaya Militsiya Street, everybody said so, but nobody knew for sure.

Eric Kraft

I CONSIDER MY LUCK

> Time and change are not optional, for the universe is a story and it is composed of processes. In such a world, time and causality are synonymous. There is no meaning to the past of an event except the set of events that caused it. And there is no meaning to the future of an event except the set of events it will influence.
>
> LEE SMOLIN, *Three Roads to Quantum Gravity*

I used to think that "Jack and the Beanstalk" was about luck, and dumb luck at that. As I remembered the tale, Jack was a dull boy, a sluggard, who complained when his mother sent him to town to sell the cow, their only remaining asset, so that they could buy some food. Whenever Jack came to mind, as he has from time to time over the years, I saw him trudging along a dusty country road, reluctantly, tugging the cow along behind him. He would rather be doing anything else; in fact, he would rather be doing nothing. That, I thought, was the essence of Jack, that he would rather be doing nothing. He had arrived at this state of mind, I had come to believe, because his past was a string of failures. Earlier, in the time before the tale that we are told, his agile mind had concocted one harebrained scheme after another, and he had thrown himself into each one with the headstrong verve of the plucky lad, and every time he had failed, because every scheme was foolish, a failure foreordained. Foolishness had made him feckless in the past, and he was feckless now for lack of trying, beaten, angry with himself, fate, the world. "I've failed so often," he moaned, "that it would be best to do nothing from now on, thereby reducing the risk of future failure to the absolute minimum." So. There he was, trudging along, sad and sullen. Why, oh why, had his mother charged him with taking the cow to market and selling it? Didn't she understand that the effort was as doomed to failure as Jack was fated to fail? He was sure to be swindled at the market, he just knew he was. The sharpers would see him coming. They'd make his head swim with their arguments and calculations, and he'd be lucky to leave with the value of a cow's tail in his pocket. The future is the name we give to our hopes and fears, and Jack felt certain that his future would be the flop his past had been.

As I understood Jack, his fear of a greater failure was what made him so willing to trade the cow for a handful of beans. A handful of beans! Not a bad bargain if you're convinced that you will lose the cow and your shirt if you go all the way to the market. Take the beans and head for home. Feel the warm flush. He did, and I imagined that he must have felt good about what he had done. He might have done so much worse.

As I understood "Jack and the Beanstalk," its essential message was that, sometimes, it's just dumb luck that gets you through. I saw it as a tale about chance, upon which so much in life, including life itself, depends. Even a gullible bumpkin can get by if he has a little luck, if the cards fall his way.

So I thought, or so I had come to think, over the years that had intervened between my last reading of the tale, as a child, and still thought when I began this book, at a time when I dearly wished that I had a cow to sell. However, my reading in bed in the time before Albertine and I turned the lights off at the end of the preceding chapter had been in the nature of research, or fact-checking. I had consulted the version of "Jack and the Beanstalk" that appears in *The Red Fairy Book,* edited by Andrew Lang, originally published in 1890. It had given me much to think about. Revisiting the source had shown me that I had been wrong about "Jack and the Beanstalk" and about Jack. I learned that Jack, far from being a sullen sluggard . . .

. . . was a giddy, thoughtless boy, but very kindhearted and affectionate.

A giddy, thoughtless boy? A boy, in short. Nothing wrong in that.
However, no evidence of the history of failure that I had come to
think preceded the opening scene. None of the brooding and sulk-
ing, none of the guilt that I had imagined. He wasn't even reluctant and fearful when he set out on the dusty road to the market:

Jack liked going to the market to sell the cow very much . . .

Ah, well. That's the trouble with checking the facts: so often it
destroys our illusions. However, if the work of memory has been
particularly mischievous in distorting them, the facts may also
bring some pleasant surprises. I was surprised, for example, to discover on re-reading (or rediscover on re-reading) that Jack was
aided in his struggles by a fairy. I picture her as long tressed and
pale, a fairy painted by John William Waterhouse. Near the end of
the tale we learn this:

Before her departure for fairyland, the Fairy explained to Jack that she
had sent the butcher to meet him with the beans . . .

Butcher! That I found surprising too, though not so pleasantly
as the discovery of the beautiful fairy. The butcher gave me pause.
The butcher made me wonder. Why should the man whom Jack
encountered along the way to the market be a butcher? Why not
a seed vendor? I grant you that it would be logical for Jack to be
seeking a butcher when he had a cow to sell, but this is a butcher
who, when he makes his first appearance on the road to the market, has "some beautiful beans in his hand." If he is a butcher, why
is he carrying beans? I've dealt with some butchers, and experience has taught me that they do not, as a rule, have beans about
them. "Not my department," they say when asked—the polite ones,
that is. Why, oh why, would the lissome, auburn-haired fairy send
a butcher to do the work of a beanmonger?

I CONSIDER MY LUCK · 89

in order to try what sort of lad he was.

Of course, of course, of course. It was a test. I was, in my re-reading, beginning to see a message in the tale different from the one that I had supposed to be its burden. Life is a series of tests, the tale told me, making it, in that respect at least, very much like school, and making school, with all its tests and quizzes and exams, ideal training for life. A test, but what sort of test? Was the fairy trying to find out whether Jack knew a bogus butcher when he saw one? Did Jack even perceive that he was a butcher? Was he wearing a bloodstained apron? Carrying a cleaver? Tattooed with the secret sign of the Guild of Itinerant Butchers? Did Jack ask himself why a butcher would be walking along the market road bearing beans? Did Jack smell a rat? Did he detect at least a whiff of rat in the air? No. He was a gullible bumpkin, like me, but being gullible didn't count against him, because the butcher and his beans were merely the start of the test, the dusty-road-to-market equivalent of breaking the seal on the exam booklet. The beanstalk itself was the real test: "If you had looked at the gigantic Beanstalk and only stupidly wondered about it," the fairy said, "I should have left you where misfortune had placed you, only restoring her cow to your mother."

Apparently, the world as run by fairies was a system not of reward and punishment but of reward and neglect. If one failed the test, one got—nothing. One was not punished. One was simply left to live as fortune's fool. (This is not to say that in Jack's world there were no imps and demons that administered other standardized tests and parceled out punishment aplenty for failure, only that fairy justice didn't work that way.)

"But you showed an inquiring mind, and great courage and enterprise, therefore you deserve to rise . . ."

Ah-ha! There it is! This is the real lesson of the tale. This is the bit of wisdom that storytelling grandparents intended to inculcate in their little lads and lasses when they told Jack's tale at hearthside on a wintry e'en. What does one need to succeed? An inquiring mind. Courage. Enterprise. These three shall see you through.

> ". . . and when you mounted the Beanstalk you climbed the Ladder of Fortune."

Interesting. Only then? Not before then? Wasn't the entire path that Jack took from the time his mother asked him to take the cow to market a part of the ladder of fortune? Why not say that he had set his foot on the ladder when he agreed to take the cow in the first place? There was some courage in that, and a bit of enterprise. No sign of an inquiring mind, I suppose. How about the moment of accepting the beans? There was some evidence of an inquiring mind there, I think, since they seemed to be extraordinary beans. Some enterprise, too, since beans are seeds, and seeds encapsulate more future value than present value, making a barter for beans an investment in bean futures, and we must be counted enterprising when we make an investment, even if we invest badly while believing that we are investing well. I see no evidence of courage in that investment, though, since Jack was, I persist in believing, trading the cow for beans to avoid humiliating himself at the market. Well, then, how about that time at daybreak when he went out into the garden and planted the beans? That shows an inquiring mind, certainly. Planting seeds and raising crops are also evidence of enterprise, the very metaphor for it, as those CEOs who promise their stockholders that they will "grow" the business while they are surreptitiously plundering it know. No courage there, I suppose. Something like timidity, in fact, creeping out before mother was up to plant the seeds unseen. So. I understand. Jack had exhibited one or two of the essential qualities before the magic moment, but only when he mounted the beanstalk did he put all three to work at once, and only then did he set foot upon the ladder of fortune. Okay. It works for me.

> After the Fairy has revealed her part in Jack's rise . . .

She then took her leave of Jack and his mother.

The fairy, I take it, represents luck. Luck, in my book, is nothing more than the name we give after the fact to an unexpected agent that initiates a string of events that runs particularly well or particularly badly. A statement about luck is a statement about the mind, not about the world. We recognize the agent of our luck only in retrospect, looking backward from a time when we feel that we have been lucky to find the moment that set off the cascade of events that brought us where we are. We expect to find a single moment, one event, a pivotal point in the history of our luck, and because that is what we expect to find, it is what we usually do find. We find what seems to have been the lucky break or the big mistake, and so we thank our lucky stars that we took the road less traveled or curse the fates that sent that little wavelet that flipped us on our backs. With hindsight, we seem to see that everything preceding the pivotal point was leading up to it, tending toward it, and that everything following it grew from it.

To any observer outside the lucky one himself, however, luck is simply chance. Chance is neutral. It is not the case that chance favors the prepared mind; it is, rather, that the prepared mind recognizes the main chance when—if—it comes. Like rain and sunlight, chance falls upon us equally, but sometimes opportunity knocks in such an outlandish fashion that only a gullible bumpkin would be likely to welcome it in. In that way, gullible-bumpkin-hood was the secret to Jack's eventual success, the preparation that led him to seize the main chance when it came along. Without the beans there would have been no beanstalk, and only a gullible bumpkin or credulous rube, like Jack, like me, would have traded the cow for a handful of beans. The fairy knew that Jack was gullible, and she took advantage of that gullibility to get him started on the path to the ladder of fortune. Has she left Jack forever? I think not. He is still a boy at the end of the tale. He still has a long way to go in life, and I would hate to think that he was going to have to make his way on his own. One's perch on the ladder of fortune is precarious. The rails are slippery, some of the rungs are missing, others are rotten. He will rise, but he will fall. Plucky lad that he is, he will scramble upward after each fall. That is, he will attempt to scramble upward after each fall. Some of his upward-scrambling schemes will be ridiculously harebrained and many of his pluckiest efforts will be feckless. Through it all, the fairy will stay with him. She will assume mortal form and become Jack's long-suffering wife. Ultimately, I think it's likely that he will settle down and write his memoirs: *The Personal History, Adventures, Experiences & Observations of Jack, the Beanstalk Boy*. Wherever he has arrived on the ladder of fortune, how high he has climbed, how far he has slipped, won't matter then. We memoirists know that we do not make life's journey to get somewhere; we make the journey so that we can tell the tale. We assist as passionate spectators at the little drama of our own lives.

Norman Lock

THE FAIRY TALE AS X-RAY OF THE WORLD
OUT OF JOINT

For a long time I scorned fairy tales, parables, and fables as children's or folk literature, as a less-evolved narrative form. I was taught this attitude. If not instructed in it, at least I came away from college with this prejudice. Who knows who or what put it there more than thirty years ago? But eventually, in my forties, I came to appreciate them. They are no longer, for me, less evolved forms but alternative ones. I have enjoyed reading them always, but I was embarrassed by the pleasure and felt I ought to be reading serious literature—*Finnegans Wake*! I now think of fairy tales, parables, and fables as serious, although their language may sometimes be rudimentary. We are reading, after all, translations from long-lost originals.

What excites me about fairy tales especially are the intimations in the text of forgotten attitudes toward the world—its dangers and forbidden pleasures. The terrors and anxieties, transmutations and sublimations. When I read a fairy tale now, I have the feeling that something is concealed—some wicked or terrible knowledge. The blood and pricked fingers, the secret nocturnal dancing, and the thickets that grow up around unconscious women. Reading a fairy tale now, I seem to see faintly what the medieval forest was—what it meant to be lost, abandoned there (a locus with symbolic, psychological, and actual, if elastic, dimensions). I feel I understand little of what is really happening inside a fairy tale. (I feel the same thing sometimes when I read Borges or try to read Eliot's

Four Quartets.) I admit that I did not discover this rich subtext on my own. I read—I don't remember where—psychoanalytical interpretations of some fairy tales; I am always keen on applying what I know of Freud's interpretations and Jung's archetypes to literature—the latter, gotten from an essay by Robert Bly in his book of poems *The Sea and the Honeycomb.* I do believe in the unconscious, believe that it enters the text during its composition— is influential on the composition—and that we can, using psychoanalytic technique, penetrate to the subtext. And should we get it wrong, there is no patient on the couch to suffer for our misguided enthusiasm.

It was in *Inventory,* a collection of essays by Michel Butor—that is where I discovered the existence of an unsuspected symbolic world within the hermetic one of fairy tales.

Parables and fables are different from fairy tales. They seem often to be depictions of the world as we know it, or at least as we know it in dreams. (I'm thinking here of S. Y. Agnon.) But their symbolic content narrows until we are left with a single signification, or meaning. The moral. When the moral is not explicit, the entire text becomes a metaphor—one of situation. That's my view of it. I like to feel that I can go through the metaphor and find something beneath. This wanting to understand is human, and art can provide us with what can be understood, through the cunning creation of a pattern, and what, finally, may not be understood. The pattern can be too highly figured, too labyrinthine. I take the difference between parable and fairy tale to be in the degree of dislocation. The fairy tale is the world at its most out of joint. And the difference between realism and fantasy lies the degree of interiority. In fantasy the world is skewed either to the idyllic or the grotesque—one an expression of desire, the other of fear. For me the difference between realism and fantasy—intelligent fantasy— is that between a photograph and an X-ray: Both are representations of reality. But which is the "realer"? The photo or the X-ray? (The answer to this question has disturbing implications for realism.)

Intelligent fantasy extends the possibilities of depiction. Using it, we can illustrate the unconscious. We can pursue questions other than those posed in the social or psychological laboratory of realistic fiction, with its emphasis on observable behavior. Fantasy's means are, of necessity, artificial in the same way that a theater production is artificial, even in the case of a naturalistic play. Art is resemblance. When the resemblance is powerful, when the artifice is successful, something happens between stage and audience, page and reader. A pact is formed. A realm of discourse established. A "reality" is negotiated. For me, intelligent fantasy is reality with its pockets turned inside out. Finally, it comes down to inclination: whether one prefers to write about the inside or the outside. Obviously, I prefer the former. But I do not exclude the latter. Together, they assemble for us a world. One which may or may not be real. Certainly, the result is real enough for most purposes.

When I think of cosmology—the extent of the universe, antimatter, black holes, dwarf stars, dark matter—I think then that nature is the greatest fantasist of them all.

The preponderance of my fiction and theater work, which are both decidedly fantastic, is influenced by the fairy-tale genre—at least by my own, perhaps idiosyncratic, appreciation of it. In *Grim Tales* I attempted to imitate the extreme dislocation of this special fictional form, to cut cloth of my own to its traditional pattern, to appropriate its narrative compression and velocity. Mine may be no more than a few sentences, although most of the 150 in the collection tend to paragraph length. In them, I express my feeling for the strangeness and mystery, the inscrutability and grotesquerie of the world. The little texts began to be written, and they seemed, in their compressed plots, sketched characters, and in their balefulness, to be like fairy tales. And they are all so grim, really—so I called them *Grim Tales,* which, of course, alludes to the great collector of German tales himself. Here is one to end on:

Each morning when he woke, he found that his papers had been worked on during the night. His affairs were being put in order—no matter how he tried to resist it, this "settling of accounts." No matter that, in desperation one night, he burnt the papers, including his last will and testament, which was now being written in a hand he did not recognize, leaving everything to his estranged wife, a woman whom he despised. Last night, having resigned himself, he took an overdose of sleeping pills, sufficient to stop his heart.

Gregory Maguire

THE WORLD TURNED UPSIDE DOWN

Thank you for bearing with me through all this, and may your *ever afters* all qualify as happy ones.

In conclusion, dear readers, let me just state again that structure turned on its head is still structure. Or, said another way, structure still is, head its on turned, structure. Forth-to-back and back-to-forth equally rely on the strong preposition "to," the preposition of intention. What have you been reading about for the past twenty minutes but precisely this?

What am I writing about now?

A silly game and I apologize, dear readers—or dearly taxed and sorely vexed readers. I won't go on expositing backward in order my points to illustrate. Glad aren't you?

One could story-tell backward, of course, and the structure would still be strong. The world turned upside down, the world turned inside out, the world turned back-to-front.

And they all lived happily ever after. But they lived in the shadow of the memory of the queen who had been obliged to dance to her death in iron shoes made red hot in the fireplace. What a strange happiness it was to live in: No one could ever erase the smell of burning flesh from the curtains of the palace. So the happiness came at a cost.

The wicked vain queen, her face distorted in its rictus, her feet charred into like two small roasted apples. How fitting her punishment had seemed at the time! But now her heirs and assigns had reason to reflect. The apple was rumored to have been poisoned, of course: it was on *that* charge that they had convicted and executed the queen. But, in fact, exactly how poisoned *had* that particular apple been? After all, Snow White had merely fallen asleep. It seemed the apple was merely narcotic—some benign soporific. After all, its effects had worn off in time. Had the queen known that would happen? Might the queen have had just cause to get Snow White out of the way without precisely eliminating her? Snow White herself, when she went to draw the curtains of a chilly October evening, caught the unmistakable reek of the queen's inflammatory end in the folds of the cloth, and had reason to question. How could Snow White find out? Was it urgent to find out? What had the queen's intention been? Didn't happily ever after mean not having to ask any questions any more?

Story will compel its structure, even when you try to subvert it. For instance, dear readers, one could start with a Q and A session at the beginning, instead of waiting till the end.

Question: As reported in the police blotter of my local newspaper, what mysterious substance, found on the floor of Crosby's Market last week, caused the management to request a police investigation?

Answer: A crushed crouton.

I haven't seen the second *Matrix* film because I'm still nursing the headache caused by the first one. But in considering The World Turned Upside Down, I quote from a *Boston Globe* article on the philosophy of Ludwig Wittgenstein and Donald Davidson on the notion that reality can't be merely an illusion, a shared—or private—metafiction for each of us.

Or maybe not a Q and A session, but to turn it upside down, an A and Q session?

Answer: Yes.

Question: Is that going to be the last mention of Wittgenstein in this essay?

I'm a novelist, not a philosopher. I will quote only one passage from an elegant, difficult essay about a movie I haven't understood.

Richard Rorty, in the *Globe,* said about the film *The Matrix:* "The hero has mostly the same beliefs *after* he is ripped out of his artificial environment as he did before. He still believes millions of the same commonplaces—the commonplaces that make it possible for him to use the same language outside the Matrix that he used inside it. He had been fooled about what was going on around him, but had never been fooled about what sorts of things the world contains, what is good and what evil, the color of the sky, the warmth of the sun, or the salient features of beavers."

Close quote.

Answer: The salient features of beavers.

Question: I didn't quite catch that: What was the final item in the list of things that Keanu Reeves hadn't been fooled about as he moved from within to without the Matrix?

The problem of language and foreignness is a crucial problem to storytellers, and few people even address it. Narnians speak in English, outside the Matrix everyone speaks in English, the White Rabbit speaks the Queen's English. In my own book, *Five Alien Elves,* when the aliens who are about to crash-land their space ship in central Vermont pick up a screech of static on their radio dials, Droyd, one of the youthful aliens, remarks, "Is that how the locals speak? I'll *never* learn the language." To which his sister, Peppa, replies, "You silly thing, you already learned the language. We're speaking it right now. Our WordSearch dials teach us any local dialect we're within brain waves of."

We seldom dream of being in places where we don't know the language, do we? We may not understand the significance of the words, but we understand the words, generally. The world can't be turned that far upside down.

Snow White found herself remembering the long dream period of her coma, when she had a bit of sweet apple caught in her throat. In fact, the very agent used to sweep her into a sleep was also responsible for her survival, for now it seemed that the queen's work with the apple had caused it to deteriorate only slowly. Sips of apple nectar drained down Snow White's throat, this minimal but essential nutrition allowing her to live. And in her dreams during that long glassy sleep! She'd been aware, sort of, that beyond her closed eyelids moved the soft blurred silhouettes of a wholly separate world. Could she only push from her coma-life, make her limbs stir, she would be through the matrix, through into a dream world, and learn it for what it was, upside down and backward, and eventually she might bring home news from the otherworld! That is, if some random randy kisser ever managed to swoop down out of the anonymous clouds and wake her up!

Question: Which one is he talking about, Snow White or Alice in Wonderland?

Answer: Yes.

"Alice took up the fan and gloves, and, as the hall was very hot, she kept fanning herself all the time she went on talking. 'Dear, dear! How queer everything is to-day! And yesterday things went on just as usual. I wonder if I've been changed in the night? Let me think: was I the same when I got up this morning? I almost think I can remember feeling a little different. But if I'm not the same, the question is "Who in the world am I?" Ah, that's the great puzzle.' And she began thinking over all the children she knew that were of the same age as herself, to see if she could have been changed into any of them."

"Mrs. Darling first heard of Peter (Pan) when she was tidying up her children's minds. It is the nightly custom of every good mother after her children are asleep to rummage in their minds and put things straight for next morning, repacking into their proper places the many articles that have wandered during the day . . ." Hmmm, said Mrs. Darling, picking up a copy of *Alice's Adventures in Wonderland* that had fallen to the floor beside Wendy's bed. Is my poppet Wendy dreaming of being Alice who is wondering if today she might not be Alice but might instead be Snow White in the glass coffin who is dreaming that Keanu Reeves is about to break through the matrix and wake her up with a kiss?

Then Mrs. Darling stood up in the center of the nursery and shook her fist straight in the face of the essayist and, without fear of waking up her darling children, she said out loud, "You'd better start making sense, Mr. FancyPants Postmodern Narrativologist, or people are going to run you out of town on a rail."

So let me start over, with apologies to the editor of this volume, Kate Bernheimer, and to anyone reading who has begun to nurse a migraine. This is a good place to go get an aspirin. I'll wait, and I'll try to be clearer below the asterisk.

*

I'm writing about fairy tales and storytelling not as a philosopher, a literary theorist, or a political pundit, but as a novelist. For every novel written for children or adults—every picture book, indeed every poem, every drawing, every work of the imagination including dreams and jump-rope rhymes—the world turned upside down is still the world, or enough of it anyway for us to negotiate with and navigate through.

I'm a fantasist by inclination, and I've made a small reputation for myself as someone who crosses the borders between children's fiction and adult fiction. Surprisingly few American writers do this, the result perhaps of excessive compartmentalization in publishing houses. Ursula K. Le Guin has managed it, of course. In her time, though I'm not certain how successfully, Madeleine L'Engle. Also, that literary lioness, Madonna. By the way, all of them are notable fantasists, one way or the other.

I started this essay with an intention to unnerve you, to cause the ground to shift a bit as you listened. To change the parameters every several paragraphs and make you uncertain. Did I also make you cross? We don't much like being uncertain, do we? Certainty is consoling, hence the appetite for all manner of fundamentalisms.

But I regret not being clear at the outset, so for a time I'll be crisply, Teutonically clear. I'll speak in sound bites. If you too had

Sister Mary Outline as your teacher in exposition and rhetoric, you can take notes. This is a capital A, Roman type, followed by a period. I'll continue when we're ready. There will be four chief areas of inquiry and a quiz worth 25 percent of your grade when we're through.

I'll go through the outline first and then elaborate.

A. FOR CHILDREN, THE ACCIDENT OF THEIR BEING ALIVE IS UPSIDE-DOWN ALREADY.

B. FICTION MAKES ITS POINTS BY SURPRISE, BUT IF THE READERS ANTICIPATE SURPRISE, THE POINT IS BLUNTED.

C. IF FANTASY WORKS AT ALL, IT IS BY JUXTAPOSING THE MIRACULOUS WITH THE MUNDANE.

D. CAN FANTASY WORK TO INTERPRET OUR WORLD WHEN IT HAS BEEN TURNED UPSIDE DOWN?

Let me go back to point A. For children, the accident of being alive is upside-down already. Every step perplexes, every attribute of the world thrills even as it alarms. That attributes exist at all is dazzling; that effects derive from causes is shocking. Oh, I lied, here's Wittgenstein again: "Not how the world is, is the mystical, but *that* it is."

From *Mirror Mirror,* my adult novel which is a saucy version of Snow White set in Tuscany in the High Renaissance of the early 1500s. The point of view is that of Bianca de Nevada, a motherless seven-year-old child living in a farmhouse on a promontory.

The world was called Montefiore, as far as she knew, and from her aerie on every side all the world descended.

Like any child, she looked out and across rather than in. She was more familiar with the vistas, the promising valleys with their hidden hamlets, the scope of the future arranged in terms of hills and light.

Once a small dragon had become trapped in the bird-snaring nets slung in the *uccellare.* Bianca watched as the cook's adolescent grandson tried to cut it down and release it. Her eyes were fixed on the creature, the stray impossibility of it, not on the spinney in which it was caught.

How it twitched, its webbed claws a pearly chalcedony, its eyes frantic and unblinking. (Despite the boy's efforts, it died, and his grandmother flayed it for skin with which to patch the kitchen bellows.)

The pertinent phrase to remember is "the stray impossibility of it." The passage concludes:

What child does not feel itself perched at the center of creation? Before catechism can instill a proper humility, small children know the truth that their own existence has caused the world to bloom into being.

So without much experience, the world might be turvy-topsy or daisy-whoopsie or downside-up, and a child can't tell: The coordinates learned from experience are not yet fixed. Nonsense is a little less so to the young. The question that Alice asks of herself in Wonderland: Am I the same person I was yesterday, and if not, who am I?—is not a nonsensical question really. If that weren't a valid question every day, it would be because we had lost faith in cause and effect. And we may have lost faith in many things, but cause and effect still has a lot of currency.

Cause and effect is still important in a fantasy. From the beginning of my children's novel, *Six Haunted Hairdos:*

"If you ever see a ghost," the boy said in a whisper, "you must do three things."

"What?" his friends asked.

"Number one. Pinch yourself to make sure you're awake. Number two: Pinch the ghost to make sure it's real."

"That's only two things," a friend observed.

"If the ghost pinches back," said Salim, "the third thing to do is *run for your life.*"

B. Fiction makes its points by surprise, but if the readers antici-pate surprise, the point is blunted.

The best illustration of this is a volume of excellent stories called *Roald Dahl's Book of Ghost Stories.* Now it's important that I said a "volume of excellent stories" rather than an "excellent volume of stories." The stories, creepy and wonderful ghost stories all, are individually memorable. But set them together in a volume advertised as a book of ghost stories and you denature them; you take from them one of the ghost story's most essential characteristics: the power to surprise. The readers end up reading each successive story for the very first instant he or she can identify the ghost. The reader is never haunted, or horrified. Surprise is vital in fiction.

Surprise is an element in the world turning upside down, of course. Were we to know it would turn, we wouldn't be shocked.

In T. H. White's *The Once and Future King,* a retelling of the Arthurian cycle that reflected mid-twentieth-century concerns about the abuses of power, the magician-tutor Merlyn lives backward in time. He explains to the Wart, who will grow up to be King Arthur:

> "Now ordinary people are born forwards in Time, if you understand what I mean, and nearly everything in the world goes forward too. This makes it quite easy for the ordinary people to live. . . . But I unfortunately was born at the wrong end of Time, and I have to live backwards from in front, while surrounded by a lot of people living forwards from behind. Some people call it having second sight."
>
> He stopped talked and looked at the Wart in an anxious way.
>
> "Have I told you this before?"
>
> "No, we only met about half an hour ago."
>
> "So little time to pass?" said Merlyn, and a big tear ran down to the end of his nose.

The reversal of Time, for Merlyn, is both the source of his mysterious wisdom and the occasion of pathos; it is the twist, the upside-down-ness, that makes yet another retelling of Arthur new and worth our time.

I was inspired by T. H. White when I wrote my adult novel *Wicked: The Life and Times of the Wicked Witch of the West.* The concept of the book itself was a reversal—that the green-skinned witch, played in the 1939 film so memorably by Margaret Hamilton, was perhaps not as bad as her reputation. But I had the fun of playing with expectations.

From *Wicked*:

> The room quieted down. Elphaba made up a little song on the spot, a song of longing and otherness, of far aways and future days. Strangers closed their eyes to listen.
>
> Elphaba had an okay voice. He saw the imaginary place she conjured up, a land where injustice and common cruelty and despotic rule and the beggaring fist of drought didn't work together to hold everyone by the neck. No, he wasn't giving her credit: Elphaba had a *good* voice. . . . Later he thought: The melody faded like a rainbow after a storm, or like winds calming down at last, and what was left was calm, and possibility, and relief.

So here I am, turning the world upside down, I hope surprising the readers who realize, with perhaps a very small lump in their throats, that, copyright considerations aside, it's clear that what Elphaba, the Wicked Witch of the West, is singing at this funeral is "Over the Rainbow." From her point of view, anyplace else would be better than Oz.

Later in my novel *Wicked,* as the Witch nears her end, she can't sleep, and she takes to drinking from a small vial of green fluid she inherited from her mother. . . . And the dreams she has, of otherworlds!

> At night she tried to train herself to look on the periphery of her dreams, to note the details. It was a little like trying to see around the edges of a mirror, but, she found, more rewarding.
>
> But what did she get? Everything flickered, like a guttering candle but more harshly, more stridently. People moved in short, jerky motions. They were colorless, they were vapid, they were drugged, they were manic. Buildings were high and cruel. Winds were strong. The Wizard stepped in and out of these pictures, a very humble-looking man in this context. In one window, in a shop from which the Wizard

was emerging rather dejectedly, she caught some words once, and willed herself with tremendous effort to wake up so she could write them down. But they didn't make any sense to her. NO IRISH NEED APPLY.

Thanks to the agency of the 140-proof miracle elixir she's glugging as well as her own natural talents, the Witch is seeing into our own world, seeing the early twentieth-century film clips of urban life, with people moving in jerky motions, on old film stock, looking colorless, drugged, manic. To her the world looks upside down. It is a shock and surprise. To us it is business as usual.

Those who meet me learn fairly quickly that I have a family; my husband, Andy Newman, and I have adopted three kids from overseas. Aware that a family with two dads is still a rather upside-down concept, we have made efforts to educate our kids early and often about theme-and-variation in life.

One day, when our oldest, Luke, was about three or four and we were anticipating the imminent arrival of his new baby brother, Alex, I was driving somewhere and chatting up the notion of family to Luke. "You have two dads," I reminded him.

"Two dads and Luke. The family."

"The family," repeated Luke dutifully.

"And now there's Alex," I reminded him. "Do you know who Alex is?"

"Alex is my baby," he said.

"No, not quite," I said, "Alex is a baby and he is your brother. You have two fathers and a brother. The family."

"The family," he said.

"I have brothers and sisters too," I said. "Do you want to know who they are?"

"No," said Luke politely.

"I'll tell you. Uncle John, Aunt Rachel, Uncle Michael, Uncle Matt, Aunt Annie, Uncle Joe. And we had a mother too. Do you know who she was?"

"Grandma?" said Luke dubiously.

"Exactly. Also we had a father but he's dead."

Luke was silent for a moment, considering, and then said ruminatively, as much to himself as to me, "Maybe a shark got him."

I reiterate: to children, the mere fact of being alive is upside-down; everything else is both secondary and possible.

C. If fantasy works at all, it is by juxtaposing the miraculous with the mundane.

Think of a bit of hallucinatory prose such as that which streams through a song like "Lucy in the Sky with Diamonds"—"Picture yourself on a boat in a river / with tangerine trees and marmalade skies / Somebody calls you, you answer quite slowly, / A girl with kaleidescope eyes." The experience of *everything* as radiantly *other* can become, in time, tiresome. As in the previous point, the absence of the virtue of surprise somewhat leeches the images of their power to astound. Yet how many wonderful moments occur in literature when a mundane moment is suddenly illuminated by a certain halogenic magic.

And she woke to find herself surrounded by seven dwarfs, each raking his beard with his fingers and shaking his knob of a head in vexation.

Mr. and Mrs. Darling and Nana rushed into the nursery too late. The birds were flown.

Alice started to her feet, for it flashed across her mind that she had never before seen a rabbit with either a waistcoat pocket, or a watch to take out of it. . . .

Or, the first line of my children's comic novel, *A Couple of April Fools:* "You don't look yourself this morning," said the farmwife to the mutant chicken.

Well, who does? As Alice pointed out, we're all different, all the time, every day.

Juxtaposing the miraculous with the mundane has to be done cautiously. Too much and you can paralyze a story. Think how slowly and carefully C. S. Lewis introduced us to Narnia: a lit lamppost in the middle of a snowy wood—and there's a faun walking by with his arms full of Christmas presents. Interestingly, that magical image was the first thing that occurred to Lewis as the story of Narnia was beginning to dawn on him. What an inspired blend of homeliness and exoticism!

With this in mind, I remember an autobiographical piece in *The New Yorker* by Gabriel García Márquez. It concerned his first published stories and the effect on his life of seeing his work in print: "I had spent almost the entire day venting my frustrations as a writer with Gonzalo Mallarino at his house on Avenida Chile, and when I was returning to the pension on the last streetcar a flesh-and-blood faun got on at the Chapinero station. No mistake: I said a faun. I noticed that none of the streetcar seemed surprised to see him, and this made me think that he was just one of the men in costume who sold a variety of things on Sundays in the children's parks. But reality convinced me that I should have no doubts: his horns and beard were as wild as a goat, and when he passed by me I could smell the stink of his pelt. With the manners of a good paterfamilias he got off before Calle 26, the street where the cemetery was, and disappeared among the trees in the park."

If anyone knows rule C, García Márquez does: If fantasy works at all, it is by juxtaposing the magical with the mundane.

D. Can fantasy work to interpret our world when our world has been turned upside down?

Here's the nub. We live in a post-9-11 world. How can any fiction make sense of things like war, like terrorism, like death on this scale, or indeed on any scale? Does fiction just crumple before the odds? For a few days, or months, did the world seem so turned upside down that fiction could no longer work as key to interpret it?

About four weeks after 9-11, my adult novel *Lost* was published. It is about a writer of fantasy whose world has gone awry due to intense grief and personal tragedy. She is unable to write, though the reader of my novel doesn't learn why until the end. Nonetheless, she considers these same questions about fiction's ability to illuminate the world. Isn't it curious how this passage, written prior to our 2001 concerns about anthrax, the collapse of buildings, etc., seems eerily prescient?

Oh, but it could be anything, anything but what it seemed to be: a figure trying to communicate through the wall at them, trying to say something, something. What was it? Beware your childhood reading, Winnie said to herself: There is no Narnia in the wardrobe, there is no monkey's paw with a third and damning wish to grant. You live in a world with starving Eritrean refugees and the escalating of urban violence into an art form. You don't need the magic world to be really real; that would be a distraction.

And the world—she stood in the hall outside John's doorway, afraid for a moment to go in—the world was already upside down or inside out; it was already Alice's mad Wonderland. . . .

A reading child back in those early days, corseted, even strait-jacketed by Victorian certainties, could delight in a story stuffed with nonsense. Time was malleable during a mad tea party in which there could be jam yesterday and jam tomorrow but never jam today. Creatures could shift shapes, a sheep into an old lady, a baby into a pig. Fury could win out over reason. In the nineteenth century, reading Alice was refreshing because it was an escape from strict convictions about reality.

But now? Now? Children in the twentieth and this early twenty-first century hated the Alice books, couldn't read them, and why should they? Their world had strayed into madness long ago. Look at the planet. Rain is acid, poisonous. Sun causes cancer. Sex = death. Children murder each other. Parents lie, leaders lie, the churches have less moral credibility than Benetton ads.

And faces of missing children staring out from milk cartons—imagine all those poor Lost Boys, and Lost Girls, not in Neverland but lost here, lost now. No wonder Wonderland isn't funny to read anymore: We live there full time. We need a break from it.

"You," said Winnie to the boot scraper hedgehog, "might as well make a statement."

The joke here is that the note that eventually will explain to Winnie where her cousin has disappeared is hidden under the hedgehog, and if the hedgehog could only have made a statement when invited to, a lot of trouble would have been avoided.

So where are we now? I advertised four points, but one of those points argued that surprise is essential. So here's a fifth notion, a final one. An extra suggestion why, if all of the above is true, we still want to read fantasy. Why the old stories like Snow White and Alice and Peter Pan deserve to be read again and again, and even, by nervy people like myself, told anew. The point is this:

E. Fairy tales and fantasy are not all that improbable as mirrors to our own world.

In effect, Winnie is wrong. We need to have experience, I think, imagining ourselves pushing through wardrobes and finding ourselves in new lands. We need to be able to imagine the otherworlds that appear when we close our eyes to sleep and dream. We need to be able to recognize when things change by the practice of imagination.

Why fairy tales? As Erik Christian Haugaard once said, "The fairy tale belongs to the poor." Even when it is about the daughter of a king, she is a daughter disenfranchised, endangered, imperiled, no more in control of her destiny than are those on hijacked airplanes or working high in magic towers. We need to practice the art of believing in survival so that when we need to survive, we recognize the concept. Why these fanciful conceits, these marmalade skies, these mutant chickens, these motherless children in fairy tales? Because by being a notch or two different than our own world, they can be noticed; they show up against the static and the smudge of dailiness. Then, when we look back at our world, we see with renewed vision, with rested eyes and restored spirits. The static isn't so impenetrable, the smudge no longer so bleary.

The last fairy tale of the piece. I grew up in Albany, New York— hardly the Bavarian woods of the Grimm tales, though grim enough, in its way. I used to work at St. Peter's Hospital while I was in Catholic high school. I would trundle the filthy linens down the utility elevators to the laundry. Each trip included three to five minutes at the elevator banks waiting for the doors to open, and while I waited, I imagined a shelf of books with my own name on their spines. I had scribbled and scrawled as a child, had read obsessively like many bright and somewhat lonely children. But it was a fantasy in my head, nothing more. A hope, an image.

As I write this in my home in Massachusetts, I swivel 90 degrees and look at the shelves in my study. Twenty-five books or more, with translations into eight or ten languages, and videos of TV movie versions, and recorded book versions in boxed sets. Why, sometimes I seem to be a fairy-tale hero myself—how improbable, with my balding pate and my thickening middle. Still, my mother died when I was born and I was raised by a stepmother. I left home to make a magical journey. It's brought me a husband, though I was expecting a wife. It's brought me my beloved children. It's brought me to Hollywood and Broadway as well as to bookstores across the land. It has brought me into the homes of thousands of readers. It is maybe thirty years exactly since I used to dream myself a future. Weren't those dreams helpful to me? I think they were.

Answer: We all do.
Question: Who gets to ask the last question?

At a used bookstore one day I noticed, behind the counter, a copy of T. H. White's *The Once and Future King* in hardcover. Shelved under a sign saying "Return to publisher," the book had a sticky label on it that said "Reads backwards." I asked to see it and bought it for two dollars. It had been bound wrong by the printer; some compositor had seen the last lines of the book, which read "*Explicit Liber Regis Quondam Regisque Futuri*—The Beginning" and had set up all 677 pages in reverse order. What I had—I trembled to realize it—was a copy of T. H. White's book that only Merlyn the magician could read, for it ran backward in time, beginning with King Arthur facing his last battle, and proceeding, left to right through all those pages, to the day Merlyn finally meets the Wart, and has only a half hour left . . .

I can't read this book, but I treasure it. The world turned upside down makes us uncomfortable, and, with luck, being unsettled may make us capable, resilient, tolerant.

This child was so beautiful that when she was born her mother died, and so the child's beginning was the mother's ending, or the mother's life can begin now, because to know who Snow White really was we must find out who her mother had been. For before the story of Snow White could start or end, there was a mother and a father, once upon a time.

As T. S. Eliot reminded us in the *Four Quartets,* dear reader, the end is where we start from. Being creatures capable both of reflection on things past and speculation on things to come, we always find ourselves, at last, right on the lip of once upon a time. And so to consider the world turned upside down, to be capable of recognizing what we have never seen before, let us start to tell stories of stray impossibilities.

Michael Martone

SEVEN DWARF ESSAYS

I.

Growing up, my son always said that when he grew up he wanted to be a seven dwarf. That was how he said it. "I want to be a seven dwarf." It was funny, of course, because he wanted the most out of that expressed desire. He wished to be both a dwarf—an interesting aspiration in itself—and all seven of the Disney alternatives at once. And this use of a singular plural could have also meant he wanted to be a whole new category of dwarf, an eighth dwarf—beyond Sleepy, Grumpy, Sneezy, etc.—while still retaining the magic completeness of the whole tribe, the one and the seven. Part of the gang but separate too. He wanted to be both uncharacteristic and characteristic at the same time. He was learning to sort by sorting. This bent had shown up quite early. In the crib he watched the floating flotilla of four stuffed bears circling above him, suspended from the twirling arms of a wind-up mobile. The bears were identical save for the different colors of their matching overalls. I cut them down when my son learned to sit up, and as soon as he could, he sat for hours, it seemed, and arranged the bears in a line—red, blue, green, yellow; green, red, blue, yellow; blue, yellow, red, green. It seemed to be in his blood, this four-letter alphabet like the code in DNA. Later it would be flags—he could recognize all the different state flags—then dinosaurs, Power Rangers, Pokémon. Even now, in the next room while I type this, the teenage version of my son has been at it for hours, arranging the song titles, the artists, the lyrics on the expanding electronic litanies of his iPod. But nothing has ever quite taken him like the Seven Dwarfs did. Not the bears or the flags or the toys or the cards or the songs. "A seven dwarf," he answered when I asked.

2.

When I was growing up, my favorite comic book was *Adventure Comics* featuring the Legion of Superheroes, kids roughly my age endowed with various powers—strength, speed, smarts. One hero could inflate and bounce. One could grow small. One could grow tall. One turned invisible. One turned into anything at all—chairs, rocks, light poles. The girl who could split into two, once could split into three. But one self had been killed long before I started reading the series. The twins treated their missing sister like a phantom limb. What I liked best was knowing that each hero had a specific weakness. Ultra Boy had ultra powers of strength, speed, etc., but could only use them one at a time. Then there were the cousins from ill-fated Krypton, Superboy and Mon-el. One could be mortally injured by Kryptonite that could be shielded only by lead; the other was vulnerable only to lead. The weaknesses and strengths were interlocking and always exploited by this month's villain. It was never the whole legion who did battle, only some subset, a team of seven, say, a line-up always shifting. Though they were heroes, those kids were freaks, of course, accurate metaphors for their teenage readers' sense of strangeness. The heroes came by their powers by accident—swept by cosmic dust, blasted by gamma rays. Or did they simply drink the wrong drink? Issue from the star-crossed combination of parents? And there is that fatalism in their genes, the chromosomes, those modern threads spun, stretched, and snipped by the three sisters. We all embody our own ancient tragedy—the very stuff that allows us to thrive as a race might well be the fatal flaw, the circumstance of our own demise. The four-handed carbons are the little gods that destroy and create. The oxygen-hungry human brain we are so proud of is an accident, and the pride the brain can conjure will be the very thing to cause our extinction. It's an old message, these fatal flaws. I remember teenage superheroes sitting around their clubhouse (they had a clubhouse!) lamenting their fates, wishing they could be like other normal teenagers of the twenty-fifth century. Or I think I remember them wishing for that. But other "normal" teenagers are never normal. Or the normalness of teenagers never feels normal. The Legion of Superheroes characters embodied the body growing up, an analog of that awkwardness. It was the theater of between-ness.

3.

"Line up!" my son commanded me, his mother, his grandparents, his babysitter. We added up to seven, and we lined up. "March!" he would then command, and we marched. The previously distributed simulations of shovels and picks were at slope arms over our shoulders. A few implements were actual scale models of picks and shovels, but some were toy golf clubs, an umbrella, a plain old stick. Outfitted, we marched. "Sing!" We sang, "Heigh Ho!" as we marched. It was this part of the movie my son returned to over and over, this going off to work. He learned very early to manipulate the remote for the VCR. He marched the Seven Dwarfs over to the mines and back, studying the formation. Disney aided the obsession by producing a videotape of excerpted songs from a variety of films in its vaults. The dwarfs marching and singing while they did so was one bit featured. We made it to the couch. "Dig!" and we dug, mining the cushions and pillows. We sang: "We dig, dig, dig, dig, dig, dig, dig, in a mine the whole day through!" And took a breath and sang: "To dig, dig, dig, dig, dig, dig, dig, that's what we like to do." I never understood the accepted conventional wisdom about attention span and the modern child. We marched endlessly. We sang for hours. We dug to China and back. It was I who always lost interest, attention waning. I called the marches to a halt, rained on the parade. The other adults, becoming self-conscious again, put down their tools, brushing the dust from their clothes. I distracted my son (who was redistributing the tools, reordering the cadre of dwarfs before him as they struggled up from their knees) by flipping on the TV, the accepted accused culprit of expanding the attention deficit, the supposed modern distraction. He scanned the tape and found the marching, the digging, and sent the images of the dwarfs back and forth on the screen. He watched as if it were the replay of the scene he had just finished staging, an actual record, not simply another version. He worked the buttons of the remote, pored over the images. Maria Montessori said that a child's play was his work—or was it a child's work is his play? In my stupor I thought it doesn't matter. It works both ways.

4.

I remember the exact moment my son transformed. It was at a school carnival, an annual event, we had attended since he was in second grade. Now he was in sixth, and although the booths and games of the fair remained constant, he was changing, literally growing, lengthening, stretching out. We drifted together over to the dunking booth. A friend of his, already wet, was on the bench, taunting the hurlers as they wound up. We watched the action side by side. Without thinking, I draped my arm around his shoulders. Instantly, I felt him tense at the touch, and immediately he began to wilt and melt away, twist out from underneath my half-embrace. It was almost botanical, leaves curling up in contact to some toxin.

In the movie Snow White mistakes the scaled-down house and furnishings she stumbles on in the forest as the habitat of children. She herself is, as they say, but a child, a child lost in the woods. Or until very recently Snow White was indeed a child. She now finds herself in the woods because one day, without her knowing it, she crossed some line from child to adult. That day the Magic Mirror's magic radar noticed that she was no longer what she had been. She became "the fairest," a code for pubescent, I suppose. Now she could be "seen." The mirror reflected that fact back to the Queen, her evil stepmother. I always ask why that day, why this one particular day. Did Snow White generate the final cell of her milky skin that morning, grow the final significant eyelash? Pubescence also suggests sprouting down or fine hair. Did the last of the downy coat sprout? Or shed? Did her lips happen to blush the proper shade of red, her eyes refract, at last, the right frequency of sparkle? Something made her euphemistically "fairest," this final part of the puzzle. One day. It was a Thursday, I guess, and the world changed. In the forest, breaking into the dwarfs' house, she mistakes it as the house of lost children. She identifies with their lost-ness. She is lost. And maybe she sympathizes with their child-ness. She herself was recently a child. She suspects however something has changed. She is no longer a child. She doesn't fit into any of the beds she finds, uses all the beds in the house for her bed. And later, when the dwarfs return from mining they peek over the beds' footboards, seven Kilroy's were here. She awakes, startled to discover that the children she anticipates are not children after all. "Why," she says, "you're little men!"

Now, I think of another moment, another scene from when my son was much younger. One day I was driving in the car. My son was strapped into his safety car seat in the back. As I adjusted the mirror, it reflected my son, stuffed into what seemed to be an undersized bucket. I was taken with how he had changed, grown larger, and I considered for a second the disclaimer printed on the outside mirrors of such reflected distortion: OBJECTS IN MIRROR ARE CLOSER THAN THEY APPEAR. But I couldn't help asking him, "When did you grow up?" Without hesitating he answered, "Night time."

5.

Living in Oblivion is a movie about making a movie. There is a dwarf in one scene of the movie being made. It is a dream sequence, and the dwarf hired to play a dwarf in the dream in the movie being made in the movie is directed to laugh. The actor asks the director for his motivation. And the director shrugs, offering only that it is a dream. After several unsuccessful takes, the dwarf finally erupts, condemning the use of dwarfs in movies, in stories. Dwarfs, he says, are always in cinematic dreams. The only work he can get as a dwarf actor is in playing a dwarf in a dream. "When you dream," he asks the director, "do your dreams have a dwarf?" The dwarf actor eyes the director, who is considering the question. "I'm a dwarf," the dwarf says, "and I don't even dream of dwarfs."

I wonder sometimes why Disney World and all the worlds of Disney are such hits. Why do certain things take, take us? Why do certain aesthetic arrangements succeed? Why, of all the flavors in the world, should a cola catch on? Why that cartoon mouse or that cartoon dog? The images created by Disney crowd out any alternative Alice or Snow White or even dwarfs. Sometimes I think it is genetic, that people are predisposed, attracted naturally, to certain combinations of things, hard wired to respond instinctually as they do to an infant, say, or a puppy. I read somewhere of Mickey's graphic evolution, his transformation from the ratlike steamboat Mickey to the high-foreheaded, big-eyed, shorter-nosed, babylike Mickey we all know. And love. Disney World is the place dying children wish for. As a last wish. Stanley Elkin's novel, *The Magic Kingdom,* even features this curiosity in its fiction. A tour of seven terminal children (their maladies roughly analogous to the Disney dwarfs' characteristic monikers—the "Sneezy" is a child with cystic fibrosis, the "Sleepy" child has narcolepsy, etc.) is trucked off to the Florida theme park. The children in the novel try to make it clear that this manufactured happiness of this happiest place on earth is not making them happy. It isn't their last wish at all. They long for a chance to grow up, of course, and seek in the sexless Magic Kingdom a chance for sex. An ultimate ride, their first and last roll in the hay. They desire to desire. They wish their illicit wish.

Disney World is a deathless place, simply enough. And I think of all the dying children who will never grow up, sentenced not only to an early death but also to an adult's version of an early death. Better to die than to grow up. There is, in the real Magic Kingdom, this studied confusion between life and death—the robots and androids, the elaborately costumed characters, the endless parades, the "cast members" sweeping, sweeping and smiling, smiling. The Main Streets ageless, frozen in time just in time.

Perhaps it was just the names. Disney was the first to name the dwarfs in the old story. No, I take that back. According to Richard Holliss and Brian Sibley in their book *Walt Disney's Snow White and the Seven Dwarfs & the Making of the Classic Film,* an English artist, John Hassall, did name them in an illustrated edition of the story in 1921. He went with domestic utensils and pantry products—Plate, Spoon, Knife, Fork, Wine, Bread, and Stool. Holliss and Sibley include the brainstorming list of names from Disney's preproduction. Scrappy, Doleful, Crabby, Wistful, Daffy, Hoppy, Soulful, Awful, Graceful, Flabby, Goopy, Puffy, Hotsy, Shifty, fifty names in all. On the list are five of the final seven. Dopey and Doc were afterthoughts, it seems. A doctor friend of mine told me she always liked Doc, of course, not just out of professional courtesy but because his is the only noun name among a legion of adjectives. The adjectives grow into nouns once they are used as names, characteristic becoming character. My son could do a pretty fair impression of Grumpy. I would egg him on. "Be Grumpy," I would say, and he would cross his arms over his chest and lower his brow and frown, pouting, tilting his head down to look at you through silted eyelids. This was his face when he was truly grumpy, when he would register his frustration, perhaps at not having the dwarfs' marching choreography go right. I was taken by the performance. I recognized myself in his clouded visage. After working for hours on a rustic portrait of the dwarfs, he would howl and destroy his work. Not right! Not perfect, and he would turn back to the same task. How silly, I thought, unable to see what he saw, unable to see the flaw in what he saw. Until I saw myself in the scaled-down drama before me, my own unself-conscious grumpiness, my idiosyncratic grumbling over a spoiled draft of an essay or story I was working on, an adult version of this play. These names, these dwarf names, are like labeled portals, doorways into adult attributes. They are gateways between these separate worlds of child and adulthood. Bashful, to me, seems the most adult, a late stage of maturation, the growing awareness of self. I am thinking of those experiments with children, their foreheads smudged with ashes without their knowing, released into a room with mirrors. Only those at a certain age will notice the smudge on the forehead in the mirror and then try to rub it off. The rest are oblivious.

6.

Growing up, my son continued to stage dramas. He acted in his high school plays. I watched him in Neil Simon's *The Good Doctor,* a play made up of seven plays based on the stories of Anton Chekhov. There is in *The Good Doctor* a continuity character named Anton Chekhov who often narrates, in a stage-manager way, the various vignettes. In the final play within a play, my son played the young Anton Chekhov, and the Anton Chekhov character took on the role of Anton Chekhov's father. The action presents the moment Anton Chekhov's father takes his son, Anton Chekhov, to a brothel on his birthday to make him a man. I sat in the high school theater surprised, a little taken aback at the maturity of the theme. My son was a freshman. I hadn't known what would transpire on stage. I had asked my son if he would like me to run lines with him while he was in rehearsal, and he had always refused. So now I watched my son take part in a depiction of a father facilitating his young son's initiation into manhood. And this construction of the drama contained within it this strangeness, this reversal of roles— the son in retrospect imagining the father at the moment the son was to become a man. I watched from the darkness. My son was very good, I thought, playing a son on the cusp of growing up. He had been in other plays. I see now he had been in plays all his life. He had started auditioning for parts in the local children's theater. He played the mysterious old man in *James and the Giant Peach* who brings the magic seeds to James. But here he was, playing a son hesitating on a threshold, a gateway concocted by his old man, who was having his own second thoughts about this initiation. But in the end the play I watched actually enacts its opposite. It takes a turn. It is a false coming-of-age story. The epiphany is that there is no epiphany. The moment of epiphany has come and gone. Instead the "father" and the "son" realize that now is not the time, that there still is time. Before they even enter it, they turn away from the brothel; they turn back home. Dramatically this turn is done with a name. Turning away from the brothel, the father calls his son back from the brink with the affectionate diminutive. "Antasha," he says, smoothing the boy's hair. My son's real name is Anthony, named for my father, though he has always gone by his middle nickname Sam. After the show I greeted him in the bright sunlight—it had been a matinee—praising his performance, his work. I was surprised by the story. I had been fooled completely, I told him. I believed everything. Outside the theater, in the sunlight, I wanted to go back in time. I wanted time to stand still. "Antasha," I said to him in his full makeup and costume, "Antasha, that was perfect."

7.

I grew up in Fort Wayne, Indiana. When I was a child, my father took me to see the dwarf houses on the north side of town. There was a little village of dwarf houses, six or seven of them, tucked within a larger neighborhood of larger houses not far from where the river curved toward the hill where Johnny Appleseed is buried. The dwarf houses looked like the regular houses around them except for their size. The houses were smaller in every regard. The scale was dwarf scale. They were bigger than playhouses. They were smaller than house houses. Their parts and the materials used in the construction—the doors and windows, porches and chimneys, the shingles and clapboards—were identical to my house, save that they were a quarter of the size. We drove back and forth on the road in front of the houses. The mailboxes on the street were the regulation-sized mailboxes, but the pole they were perched upon was thigh high. My father pointed out how big the meter boxes looked, how the cars parked in the driveway were like regular parked cars, how the silver propane tanks, well, dwarfed the houses like zeppelins moored to their hangars. I suppose we were waiting to see who would emerge from the tiny doorways to check the mail or pick up the paper or water the postage-stamp-sized lawn. We never did catch sight of any of the inhabitants. My father had heard that this was a winter camp of traveling performers. The houses were empty most of the year, the owners on the road with carnivals and sideshows. But even that we were never able to really prove, probably an urban legend. I took my son to see the dwarf houses. He was then the age I had been when my father first took me to see the dwarf houses. It was Christmas, and there were little icicle lights hanging from the miniature eaves, halfway down the side of the houses. You know the feeling when you return to look at the houses you grew up in or when you haunt the neighborhoods of your childhood, you have the sensation that everything is smaller—the houses, the trees, the lawns. Memory gives you a map more detailed than the original. The original is underwhelming, shrunken, contracted, lacking. But visiting the dwarf houses I had visited again turned out all different. The dwarf houses seemed larger than I remembered them. I drove with my son back and forth around the little grid of narrow streets lined with the dwarf houses. There were lights on, and the Christmas decorations twinkled. The walks had been shoveled and the snow piled up into piles. Smoke seeped from the chimneys. We didn't see anyone. So I drove over to my old neighborhood to show my son the tiny, tiny house where I remember growing up.

Michael Mejia

NOBEARD

> What interests us in the character of Gilles de Rais is generally what
> binds us to the monstrosity that a human being harbors since tender in-
> fancy under the name of nightmare.
>
> GEORGES BATAILLE, *The Trial of Gilles de Rais*

Bedroom

There were break-ins in the neighborhood. A man lingering in the
backyards, in darkness and daylight.

Some time has passed since then, and my wife tells me that the dog
was up barking last night. He was standing on the edge of the bed,
barking into the darkness, at the empty doorway. I don't recall any
of this.

—I was asleep, I say.

—He was barking at your cats, she says. And by cats she means
rats. We don't have rats. We have something and it periodically dri-
ves the dog wild. He runs into the hall and snuffles and scratches
at the baseboards and the defunct floor registers. He growls and
barks and eventually gives up, wears out the routine, comes back
to bed.

But last night was something else apparently. The darkness was there and he barked at it from the edge of the bed.

Library

The book has an orange library binding with a creature, perhaps a goblin, imprinted in black on its spine, and the name of the book is something like *Folk and Fairy Tales from around the World*. It is the only book I check out repeatedly from the library of John Cabrillo Elementary School in Sacramento, California.

The John Cabrillo Elementary School library is small and intense. Books line three walls, and there are short, two-sided stacks in the center of the room as well, and child-sized chairs and tables. It is like a dollhouse library. Even the librarian does not seem quite real, as though she is play-acting for us, preparing us for meeting a real librarian out there in the other world beyond the emerald-leafed hedges.

I never finish the book.

Later, after I've discovered *Folk and Fairy Tales from around the World,* and perhaps after I've stopped checking it out repeatedly, though I've not yet forgotten the power of one particular story in it, a friend, or rather an acquaintance, a boy whom I will eventually come to dislike, shows me a photo in another book. A young mother preparing to breastfeed her child. A close-up, in black and white, covering two oversized pages and a circle drawn around the mother's exposed nipple in black ballpoint.

—Look at this.

I don't understand.

—Didn't your mother breastfeed you?

I don't know. So I ask. My mother seems uncertain. Perhaps she is shocked. She says no. I'm not sure that I believe her now, though I did then, and I am advised not to look at such pictures, not to talk to such people. Too late.

Only One Story

I recall only one story from *Folk and Fairy Tales from around the World*. It is the story of Bluebeard. I'm not even certain now if that is what it was called in this book, but I am certain that this is the story. A young woman, a princess, marries a wealthy man to whom she does not want to be married because he frightens her. He has had several wives before her, perhaps they were even her sisters. On their wedding night, the fearsome husband gives her the keys to every door in his castle and tells her what each one is for. The final key, he says, goes to that little door at the top of the stairs. You must never open that door or I will be very angry. The husband goes away on a trip and the princess, bored, wanders his immense castle, opening every door with the keys she's been given. She is amazed by her husband's wealth but soon tires of every pleasure until she gets to the final door. She opens it and discovers a filthy closet covered in gore. The dismembered bodies of all her husband's previous wives, perhaps her sisters, are there, and she realizes that, now that she has seen it, she will be next. The husband returns. She is doomed. Somehow she escapes and lives happily ever after.

Perhaps the story is familiar, or parts of it, anyway. I have tried to paraphrase it as I remember it from that first reading, trying to keep it as free as possible from subsequent versions I have encountered elsewhere. Regardless, what I recall in particular from that first version of a story that will continue to haunt and inspire me are these things:

> The bride's fear
> The transaction with the keys and the husband's admonishments

The bored, abandoned bride wandering the castle
Her fear giving way to wonder
The horror of the filthy closet
The happy ending

I'm not certain how many times I re-read that story, but I know it was several, that that story in particular is what drew me back again and again to *Folk and Fairy Tales from around the World*. No other story seemed to hold the kind of power that one did, and perhaps that's why I never finished the book.

Bedroom

I have my own turntable now and Bartók's only opera is playing on it. His strange polytonality and Béla Balázs's ambiguous libretto are transforming my favored image of Bluebeard into a monolithic Slav, into Kékszakállú. "Bluebeard" is a cartoon. "Barbe-Bleu" also isn't quite right. Too refined. I prefer the German "Blaubart" with his brutal, final *t*. But now this Kékszakállú, both lyrical and savage. His need is inexplicable. He is a deep reservoir of terror that has no reason. Kékszakállú is as haunted as I am by his warning, yearning love song: *Judit . . . Judit . . .*

Library

Still later, I am writing a story about Blaubart, a charmless, chintzy magician, the washed-up scion of a line that extends back to Cagliostro and St. Germaine to clans from the Carpathians to the sorcerers of the Egyptian New Kingdom. Bluebeard as has-been, as schlub, wifeless, harmless, tragically heroic. Bluebeard without the filthy closet. The story too is a failure. But in the process my Bluebeard continues to accrete his crust of camp and horror. In the stacks I discover Bataille's book on Gilles de Rais. Once considered a hero for having served in the company of Jeanne d'Arc during the Hundred Years' War, Gilles was later tried and executed in 1440 for the sadistic murders of hundreds of children, mostly young boys, whom he kidnapped or otherwise had procured for him and then sodomized. In some cases they were sacrificed in occult rituals. While there is no connection, Gilles has sometimes been considered the inspiration for the Bluebeard legend popularized by Charles Perrault in the 1690s. Bataille's is a book of true crime, true horror. Gilles is the filthy closet multiplied.

Living Room

The living room is not a room for living. It is a room for working. Sometimes it is a room for play. Sometimes the play occurs around the stacks of his books my father has removed from the shelves and placed in careful piles on newspaper to protect the carpet while he meticulously dusts the volumes, shakes them, and returns them to their place. These stacks are the site of my brother's urban warfare activities, green plastic men and materiél. The living room is a place of business and play. It is a place where things can stand unmolested and gather dust. It is a place where the Christmas tree stands after everything has been put away, rearranged, secured. The turntable plays the Beatles, Fleetwood Mac, Sesame Street, Bing Crosby, and Mario Lanza singing Christmas carols.

The living room is also a library. Most of my father's books fill shelves on one wall. And across the room there is another, octagonal set of shelves containing even more books that he acquired during his time in college and in the navy.

Look at this.

My brother introduces me to my father's *Bluejackets Manual,* a guide to knots, fitness, signaling, small arms training, and the care and maintenance of facial hair, among other things.

KTXL Sacramento

Joey Heatherton is in bed, luxurious ivory sheets pulled up to her neck. Richard Burton, neatly goateed, lies next to her, on top of the sheets, his hair a stiff, blue-black wave. Joey has asked Richard a question and Richard is telling a story. The sound is down and their murmuring seems more sexualized than is common at this time of night. They live in the lurid, oversaturated colors of early 1970s European cinema.

—Camp, someone says.
—Soft porn, says another.

And now the channel has been changed.

Monstrosity

The monster is vision that will not turn away. The monster is what we are not, what we cannot be. And in our innocence we are ignorant, a state we cannot bear, that has the feeling, finally, of monstrosity.

Interlibrary Loan

This is not the film I wanted. I requested Dymytrk's *Bluebeard* (1972), starring Richard Burton as the murderous Baron von Sepper, Joey Heatherton as Anne, Raquel Welch, Virna Lisi, Nathalie Delon, Marilù Tolo, Karin Schubert, Agostina Belli, the voluptuous murdered brides. But I allowed for other editions and Dymytrk's did not arrive.

So, instead, my wife and I are watching Ullmer's *Bluebeard* (1944). John Carradine, sans beard, plays Gaston Morrell, a painter and puppeteer, a murderer of beautiful young women, his models, who keep turning up strangled in the Seine. He is given the name Bluebeard, or The Bluebeard, by a terrified French populace unaware of his true identity. Morrell's motives (there must always be a motive for murder, n'est-ce pas, reason and logic in the crime thriller?) remain enigmatic for much of the film until, finally, he reveals that what set him off was the failure of an ideal, the failure of a waif, Jeanette, for whom he cared once, when he found her ill in the street, and whose seeming purity inspired his painting of the Maid of Orleans (dimly Jeanne and Gilles continue to haunt the tale), his finest work. When the painting won an award, he visited Jeanette, to share the good news, but she turned out, as he says, to be a "low, coarse, loathsome creature," and this failure of character compelled him to murder her. Each subsequent model only reminds him of this betrayal and so they too must die.

My wife asks me to rub her shoulders. My hand comes down on her neck and we laugh until I begin, unintentionally, too hard.

Two Questions I Have Never Asked

Why is your beard blue?
Why am I terrified of a blue beard?

Unreason

I am not satisfied with Bluebeard as murderer or madman, as one who can or would testify before a culture that considers him criminal. Perhaps this explains the poor fit of a Morrell or a von Sepper or a de Rais. Kékszakállú has no mechanism for explanation. To explain would never occur to him, and he would not comprehend the concept. He exists only in the process of his . . . careful now: to call these "murders" or "crimes" continues to apply the language of the law. Rituals, doses, consummations, transformations, metamorphoses: Kékszakállú's deeds are the inevitable reciprocations for our wanting to know.

Portrait

No Van Dyke or Goatee or Hulihee. No Muttonchops or French Fork or Franz Josef. More like the coarse pelt of a massive, unknown beast, a blue-black beard like a robe, concealing any detail of him you might take to be human. The eyes, too, are from another world. In them, you, puny, are prey. You are skinned alive.

Bedroom

I am dreaming or I am not. The dark shape stands motionless in the doorway. What does he want? What is he waiting for? The motionless figure observes me helpless.

Closet

Standing on the threshold of the filthy closet, eyes adjusting to the bloody darkness, we are reaching out eagerly for the unreadable. The attractive power of the Bluebeard legend lies not in Bluebeard, a mechanical agent of destruction, but in our desire to enter the filthy closet from the very moment it appears on the page. The shocking orderliness of its horror—wives hung on the walls, severed heads arranged as in a boutique—is reflected in the law of Bluebeard, a law we read as criminal, but to which we, with the little bride acting as our avatar, submit nonetheless for the sake of an evolutionary terror, for the sake of the unexperienced pleasure.

Kitchen

—Didn't your mother breastfeed you?

I ask my mother about this. She says nothing and immediately I am ashamed. I have introduced something uncomfortable, alienating, between us, perhaps the first such thing I can recall, and I know that this is not good. I am not good. I am encouraged to make friends with good people, to make better friends. This boy whom I will come to despise, most likely for showing me this photo, for giving me something to introduce into my relationship with my mother that is uncomfortable, is not good.

Some years later I am good, and I will be commended for making good choices in friends, for choosing friends who are good. They are good and I am good. Why, I wonder, have I been so good?

. . . . unbound to the limits of ordinary life . . .

Bataille is speaking here of Gilles, of his transformation from human into legend, into a so-called sacred monster, a saint of excess, into Bluebeard. The metamorphosis is necessary, inevitable, because we cannot allow that such monstrosities could really be perpetrated by a human being.

But the desire to be unbounded. This too was Gilles's desire. And can't we say the same of the bride of Bluebeard, who convinces herself that his beard is perhaps not so blue, not so fearsome after all; and of Balázs's Judit, who comes to Kékszakállú's weeping castle despite the rumors she has heard? The desire for the singular, to make the unique discovery, the discovery that surpasses reason and evolves us, is why we want that key, want only to be shown the steps leading up to the forbidden door, for dear Kékszakállú to go on his way and let us fail at our leisure.

Perhaps this singularity is the source of Bluebeard's fearsome mutation, the color of his beard the reflection of the horror he now sees all around him, everything stained with blood, the bodies of that ordinary world turned inside out, the invited visitor, the wife as a body in need of decapitation. And this is the new threshold of the monster, what we don't want to understand: How does one begin to see the world anew? What are the risks, even if we could conceive of such a way of seeing, if we could imagine—and yes, oh yes, we can—if we can imagine this, if we were to one day awake and see this way, what happens to us, to that so-called ordinary world? Is the little bride made monstrous now by what she has seen? Can we believe that she will now return to herself once she's left Bluebeard's castle?

Sexual Terror

By this perhaps one might mean a fear of the unimaginable, the unimagined, of the most unexpected uses of the body, one's own or another's. And once the threshold of that terror has been passed, perhaps it is transformed into a terror of what cannot be regained or of what more can be discovered.

Living Room

Look at this.

I am older now and home alone, wandering the house in Sacramento. Now I am looking through my father's books. I see some stacked behind the rows at the front of the octagonal shelves and I pull them out. Among them I find one with a light blue library binding, something to do with sex, a clinical title, a how-to title. At this time I do not know how to. Not really. It is a book of a certain era that has passed. But not passed out of the house.

In the book I find a line drawing of the vagina. It appears in the midst of an explanation of foreplay. I do not recall the details of the explanation, but I do recall the words "white hot." This is a level of excitation one wants the female to achieve before concluding foreplay and moving on to intercourse. These are the terms of this particular classroom. Politely lurid. I never read the book. I do not sneak it to my bedroom, hide it under the mattress, anything like that. I return it to its place, that *white hot,* that line drawing stuck with me now forever. I return the wall of books that defend this knowledge and feel, yes, a little ashamed.

The line drawing is hairless.

This Story

In this story, I am not Bluebeard. I am no murderous lothario. I am not a wife killer, a serial murderer, serial seducer. No strangler or butcher. Not one who destroys out of vengeance, disaffection, or impotence. I am no sociopath, no misanthrope, no tragic beast who exits the woods only long enough to lure a bride back to his weeping castle and then . . . I do not dream of decapitations, am not lured by the blood of others.

Am I, then, the little bride in this story? Both fearful and ambitious, curious, wandering the castle alone while my brutal husband awaits my misstep, hunts me in what is now my own home whose wonders, without opening that door, I will soon exhaust? Should I just lie still in the bed, then, and await his return, pretend the key is not in my hand, warming with my blood?

Bedroom

I am listening to the darkness. I am looking into the bedroom, listening for signs that my wife is waking up, that she is ready for coffee. And then the dog is up and barking. The dog is barking at me, the dark, still shape in the doorway.

Timothy Schaffert

A LANGUAGE OF TOADS

Our new dogs would dig up bones then bury them again in the field, the bones, I presumed, of the old dogs we'd seen die. Pooch and Snow, husband and wife, had failed to make it through one bitterly cold winter, and my father had buried them in the same square of ditch he'd buried snakes he assassinated for me in the garden. (The sight of a snake so legless in the shade of the low leaves of the pumpkin patch would send me running, and I wouldn't return to the garden until I saw the snake hanging limp, all its mocking wiggle gone, from the end of my father's hoe.) I'd been young enough when Pooch and Snow were old that I'd seen them as elegant somehow, dignified royalty despite their wolfish taste for chasing the rabbits that they'd sometimes catch and tear away at until they were nothing but pretty tufts of fur.

The bones on our farm were likely not the bones of dead dogs but ones only tossed into the yard from the kitchen, the remnants of a Sunday night roast or Saturday night steak. But once anything entered the out of doors, it took on, to me, a sinister touch. Sickly, pale, and not at all sporty, with a paranoid imagination that sometimes left me crippled by a baseless fear, I was not the farm boy my parents had expected. I was distracted and uneasy, and I could lose myself, beyond all good sense, in storybooks.

In the basement of the library in town, a librarian named Mrs. Mulligan stood guard over the children's collection, her thick-heeled shoes noisy on the wood floor as she clomped around, shushing at the slightest squeak, her finger lifted, coarse hair curling up from her knuckles. Once, my friend Sarah and I crept over to the fifth-grade's section to pore over the illustrations in a book on human reproduction. Our giggling grew so raucous, it attracted Mrs. Mulligan, who suddenly appeared at the end of the row of stacks, her gaze falling onto the page open to the source of the hilarity—a drawing of a naked man and woman assuming the missionary position. Sarah and I clammed up, and I was certain we were about to be plucked from the library, our cards revoked, our parents alerted. Perhaps we'd even lose the very sexual organs we'd just learned all about. But Mrs. Mulligan, taken aback for the first and only time I'd ever witnessed, simply told us to be quiet, and she stepped away, rendering our dirty book, in one fell swoop, blandly innocent.

A few weeks later, Mrs. Mulligan, perhaps because of her awareness of my sexual exploration, refused to check out to me the illustrated fairy tales I'd selected. I was too old for them, she explained, and she thrust upon me a book about the Bobbsey Twins at the ocean. I spent that week in despair, the book open and unread before me, as I looked over its cover and out the window at a farm as landlocked as any there was.

In the country, where seeds are nestled and nursed in spring, musk thistle and fanged worms poisoned in summer, the overgrown world of fairy tales, with its knowing beasts and spindly trees, seems strikingly down-to-earth. And winters on the farm are just as dead and white as those that plagued the impoverished in the stories of the Grimms. Though I never believed for a moment in the magic of the stories, in the way that I believed in the magic of the Bible, the tales seemed rich with truth, their morality complex and, at times, indecipherable. I never knew what to make of the version of "Hansel and Gretel" that I knew best. I'd thought it arrogant of the children to start gnawing on the doorknobs and shutters of a stranger's house, not to mention potentially dyspeptic, and they should have expected a trap. When I wasn't feeling superior to the children, I was feeling inferior, afraid that, in similar circumstances, I wouldn't have had the foresight to present a pigeon bone to the blind witch when she came to my cage to pinch my finger and check on my level of plumpness.

But none of that changed the fact that I could picture Hansel and Gretel scattering breadcrumbs in the minor orchard outside our backdoor. There was no way to get lost among these haphazardly planted crabapples and black walnut trees, lilac and rose bushes, but when ignoring the miles of flat emptiness that crept up to the edge of this minute forest, I could picture the woods as without end.

And within this thicket of trees was an old, forbidding house. I grew up in a ranch-style home painted blue, built the year before I was born; before that, my parents and two older brothers had lived in an old farmhouse that had yet to be torn down despite its treachery. I always longed to step inside and pretend to live in its rooms. My mother had told stories about the misery of the house, how icicles formed on the walls in the winter and a bitter wind whistled through cracks in the glass of the windows. The house, though it had been abandoned for only a handful of years, was determined too weak for even a tour on tiptoe. I never saw inside until I was a teenager, when the house was torn down to make room for a building to hold farm implements. First, a single wall dropped away, and before the rest of the house of sticks collapsed to the ground, I studied this cross-section from across the yard, picturing my young mother and young father in their pajamas on Christmas, as old photographs had portrayed them, a sweet little family I had never met. I scrutinized the yellow roses in the wallpaper pattern and the threadbare wine-colored rug that dotted the stairs with fleur-de-lis, memorizing all I could in the few minutes left of the house's existence.

There were other structures on the land, a ghost town of failed farm projects. The chickens had long since flown their rickety coop, and one summer all the hogs in the hog shed had died, one by one, struck down by contagious disease. Another shed was furnished with castoff tables and chairs, every piece gray with thick dust and draped with the silk of long-undisturbed cobwebs. It was in that shed that my friends and cousins and I staged fairy-tale theatricals; a favorite was the story of Snow White—a crumbling vanity with a round, fly-specked mirror provided the perfect prop.

For me, much of the drama of a fairy tale rests in such props: a poisoned apple with one toothy bite missing, a spinning wheel, a radish stolen from a garden, a glass slipper, a glass coffin, a windowpane of sugar, a spindle, a shuttle, a needle. The plots held little interest, too full of mayhem and hinging too much on a character's gullibility, the tales too antique in their logic. So we often created our own plots from what props we could find on the farm. One afternoon I led my school friend Sarah from the shed, taking from it the leg off a broken porcelain doll. We crawled through the barbed wire of a fence (though we could have opened the gate) in order to pull an unready carrot from the ground. We headed then to the woods, stopping for a moment at the edge of the pasture. Sarah took a piece of broken brick and threw it at a cow, hitting its head. I was terrified she'd killed it, and we stood there for several minutes, watching the beast, waiting for it to keel over or to at least register the pain. I felt bad for the cow, and in my mind Sarah became the wicked stepsister of our impromptu tale.

In the wood was a stump that reached up to my waist, and it became my pulpit, from which I preached of the dangers facing Little Red Riding Hood. Sarah, looking through a View-Master, aiming it up toward a slant of sunlight, followed along with the story, clicking the wheel forward, picture by picture, Little Red's fright in 3D, her bottle of wine frozen in the air as it fell from her basket, spilling.

On the schoolyard, miles from our parents on their farms, sex became part of the theater. Usually I was the only boy who'd play with the girls, so I'd be cast as every prince, and we'd continue each story beyond its happily-ever-after ending. One rainy day I kissed Sarah at the end of a wedding ceremony beneath a clear plastic umbrella, and then we honeymooned. We lay on the wet ground, and she lifted the bottom of her dress far above her dirty knees. I held out my hand, from which she took a blue juniper berry I'd plucked from the branch of a fir tree, and she touched it to her tongue and pretended to eat it. Together we drifted off into a mock slumber. On our backs, on a soft patch of grass, we looked up at the rush of the gray clouds, as a gaggle of maidservants hid behind a hedge and laughed. Then, when we woke from our years of sleep, our fairy tale became a portrait of domesticity, devolving into the world we knew better, and we reenacted the mundane, our maids changing roles, becoming our children whom we scolded and punished for their invented naughtiness, spanking them lightly with switches broken from a bush.

Sarah visited the farm again one summer afternoon. While our mothers had Coke and ice cream at the kitchen table, Sarah and I decided to fathom the depths of "Toads and Diamonds."

"Toads and Diamonds" was the fairy tale that mystified and fascinated me the most. I'd only ever seen it in one book, a cheap slim *Blue Book of Fairy Tales,* with cardboard covers, bought at the grocery store and featuring pale illustrations, all the characters drawn with black dots for eyes and tiny lines to show where their cheeks sunk in. In the story two grown stepsisters live in a cottage in the woods. The mother is partial to her foul-tempered, dark-haired daughter and lets her be lazy, while her sweet, blonde stepdaughter must do all the housework. The blonde daughter is sent to the village to collect some water from the well, where she meets a thirsty old woman begging for a drink. The blonde gives her a sip from a vessel. The old woman confesses to being a fairy, and she rewards the girl's generosity with a magical spell: whenever the girl speaks, diamonds and pearls and rosebuds roll off her tongue. When the girl returns home, the stepmother is so impressed, she orders her ill-mannered daughter to take a pitcher to the well herself, in search of the old woman. But this time the fairy takes the form of someone of elegance, and the dark-haired daughter refuses her a drink. The fairy curses her, and from then on, whenever the dark-haired one speaks, toads and snakes slither from her lips.

The oppositeness of it all appealed to me but not as yet another good versus evil allegory. I got enough of the battles between God and the devil in church, leaving nothing ambiguous in my mind.

I was so frightened of hell that I chanted to myself several times a day, my hands clasped and my eyes shut tight, promising the Lord that I believed in him. Compared with the floods and plagues of locusts and turnings-to-salt artlessly illustrated in Sunday school workbooks, the plight of the sisters, and their conflicts, seemed almost whimsical and refreshingly unbelievable. I had actually wanted the story to continue, as Sarah's and my fairy-tale wedding had, into the realm of the day to day. I wanted to know what kind of life such a blessing and a curse could offer the sisters. Did the good sister open a jewelry shop and make a fortune, or did the constant flow of diamonds and pearls at the slightest whisper torture her, become a wicked currency? And as much as I hated snakes, I somewhat envied the bad sister's powerful invective.

For our production of "Toads and Diamonds," my mother loaned Sarah a dress she'd worn only once: a countrified gown of rickrack and lace that she'd stitched together for the town's centennial celebration. It had been a short dress on my mother but flowed long and luxuriously down Sarah's legs. My family spoke of the centennial fondly and often, and there were photographs in our albums of everyone in hats and boots on their way to dances and parades. That may have been the source of my first true pangs of regret—that I'd been born a year too late for the weeklong party. Not only had my mother made a dress, but my father had won a beard-growing contest.

Sarah and I walked past the woods and across the cornfield to collect baby toads from the edge of a creek. Though I hated snakes, I loved to make the tiny toads leap away from me. Feeling dramatic in her long dress, Sarah sat on the bank of the irrigation pond and abandoned the production. But as she rubbed the mud from the shell of a snail, and I practiced skipping rocks, we discussed "Toads and Diamonds" and its complications. In the story's end, the sister who speaks in diamonds and pearls attracts a marriage proposal from a handsome prince, an unlikely development in our opinion.

"If she sighed a little when he frenched her, he'd end up choking on a diamond," Sarah said, and I nodded and rubbed my chin in a manner that I imagined to be thoughtful. Only months before, at the mere mention of frenching, Sarah and I would have split our guts with laughter. But our love affair was in decline. That afternoon was Sarah's last on the farm, and when our mothers called to us from across the field, we ran to them, so relieved to not be left to our own resources. No cunning sea creatures had coiled up from the murk of the irrigation pond to molest us. No pack of wolves in tuxes and wingtips had attempted to seduce us with martinis and cute swizzle sticks. All the sublime terrors of adulthood remained blessedly out of reach.

David J. Schwartz

ON MAKING NOISE
Confessions of a Quiet Kid

This is a story about noise.

I am the product of a mixed marriage between a Norwegian Lutheran farm girl and an Irish-German Catholic boy from St. Paul. The boy and the girl got married and lived happily ever after in the city (and, later, the suburbs) with their four children.

I don't remember it, but I know that my dad used to read me stories of Robin Hood and King Arthur, much as his older brother had done for him. I know this is true because later, when I read those stories myself, I already knew them.

Two things happened soon after this, while I was still very young. Three siblings were born in quick succession, and my father went to night school so he could make the money to pay for all of us. Our father-son time went away. My mother, left with the four of us, made Dad the bogeyman of her attempts at discipline: "When your father gets home . . ."

My father has mellowed over the years, but there was a time when I was terrified of his temper. Spankings were de rigueur in our household, and as the eldest I got plenty of them. I learned the lessons. No fighting. Table manners are important. Keep the noise down. Strangers in restaurants used to compliment my parents on how quiet and polite we were. My mother's standard response was to laugh and say, "That's because their father is a grouch."

I was not only quiet, I was shy. There were other children in our neighborhood, but I had to be coerced out of the house, away from my books and toys. Play was very serious, and other children were likely to make a mess of it with their silliness. I was, in many ways, a far more serious child than I am an adult.

My mother's parents lived three hours away, and although it feels like we visited often, in reality it couldn't have been more than once every couple of months. There were things I liked about the farm—I loved Grandma and Grandpa's dog, Prinny, and the cows, and the barn was huge and scary and fascinating. But I was allergic to everything, and in the end I preferred the company of books. I was probably eight or nine when I discovered—or perhaps Grandma showed me—a box of comics that had belonged to my uncles. Also inside the box was a copy of *Grimm's Fairy Tales*.

I read the comics first. What can I say? They had pictures, and we didn't have comics at our house. But at that time they struck me as a little—well, silly. Alternate Earths were silly, as were the apparently endless random effects of Red Kryptonite. I came back to comics when I was older, but for the time being I put them down and picked up the *Grimm's*.

I knew some of the stories, of course. At least, I knew the Disney versions. Besides the features, Disney made a series of shorts based on fairy tales, most starring Mickey Mouse as Jack or the Brave Little Tailor or some other intrepid. *The Wonderful World of Disney* was regular viewing in our house, and I'd seen those versions many times. They were pretty silly, though. I knew the difference between real and imaginary, and it was very simple: cartoons were not real, and everything else on TV was. No one told me this—I just knew it. The people were real, and they couldn't all be liars. There were gray areas in this cosmology, though. The Muppets, for instance, were clearly real, but I wasn't as certain about H. R. Pufnstuf. But *The Monkees* was a documentary series, and *Doctor Dolittle* (the Rex Harrison version) was proof that animals did talk.

(To me there was no contradiction in thinking that Pushme-Pullyu was real but Mickey and Goofy were not. The Disney characters didn't even act like animals, except perhaps for Pluto—but Pluto was just Goofy on four legs, minus the beatnik getup. These talking characters had no relation to the animals on the farm or the dogs at home. I'm not even sure I realized that Mouse was anything other than a surname until later.)

So talking animals made sense, but other things in *Grimm's* did not. I didn't for one second believe in pumpkins that became coaches or giants who came down beanstalks. People didn't turn into swans, and babies were not born the size of thumbs. I knew these things with a certainty that I no longer possess. I didn't have much patience for most of the stories, but there was at least one exception.

"The Bremen Town Musicians" begins this way, or at least it does in the edition I found in that box of comics:

> A certain man had an ass which for many years carried sacks to the mill without tiring. At last, however, its strength was worn out; it was no longer of any use for work. Accordingly its master began to ponder as to how to best cut down its keep; but the ass, seeing there was mischief in the air, ran away and started on the road to Bremen; there he thought he could become a town-musician.

This was all perfectly sensible. Animals worked on farms, obviously. That was their job. As for becoming a musician, it struck me as a bit impractical, but then the Monkees were a band and they seemed to be doing all right. I approved of songs, in any case.

What followed made perfect sense as well. The ass met an old hound who could no longer keep up with the pack, a cat too old to catch mice, and a rooster destined for Sunday soup. He invited them all to join him on the road to Bremen. Obviously he was putting the band together. I can still picture the ass wearing that same stocking cap that Mike Nesmith used to wear on every episode of *The Monkees,* a habit I tried to emulate until my mom told me we didn't wear hats in the house in the middle of summer.

It was apparently a long way to Bremen. Late at night, cold and hungry, the animals saw a light in the forest and went to investigate. They found a house full of robbers enjoying a feast. Robbers were another thing I knew to be real. Sometimes I lay awake listening for them. If they came, I planned to drive them away with one of the sticks that I had smuggled into my bedroom. Afterward my parents would weep in gratitude and beg forgiveness for ever having spanked me.

I was curious as to how the animals would handle the robbers; I wanted to compare strategies. Quoting again:

> The ass was to take up his position with his fore-feet on the window-sill, the hound was to jump on his back, the cat to climb up onto the hound, and last of all the cock flew up and perched on the cat's head. When they were thus arranged, at a given signal they all began to perform their music; the ass brayed, the hound barked, the cat meowed, and the cock crowed; then they dashed through the window, shivering the panes. The robbers jumped up at the terrible noise.

Noise.

The robbers flee, and the animals lay claim to the house. Later, a lone robber returns to scout them out, but in the darkness the animals become the bumps in the night—the cat becomes a witch in his retelling, the dog a man with a knife, the ass a monster with a club, and the rooster a judge calling down a sentence of doom. The musicians settle down in the house they have won by noise and live there for the rest of their days.

I don't know if I can explain how transgressive this was to a quiet child. The idea that noise might be a *good* thing—it was confusing and troubling. It seemed somehow wrong for this to be in a book for children. But tentatively I began to test this radical tactic. Late at night, when the darkness and silence ran out of things to whisper about and turned their attention to me, a sharp cough sent them scattering back to the corners of the room. A restless creak of bedsprings warned the thing under the bed not to reach up. But the idea of making a purposeful noise was too radical. To be seen and heard at the same time, to call attention to the fact that I was a child, was terrifying.

I was too mature to be a child, too awkward and ignorant to be a grownup, so books and records were my best friends. I read quietly, the radio tuned to easy listening. I stayed serious; although I eventually moved from juvenile mysteries to fantasy novels, they were *serious* fantasy novels; thick books, fate-of-the-world stuff. I had no time for nonsense.

Until, sometime in junior high, it all flipped. Suddenly the dour and mannered worlds of Tolkien and C. S. Lewis were juvenile; the safe sounds of Air Supply and Barry Manilow no longer soothed but grated. The complexities of polite behavior were arbitrary rules passed on by people long dead. Suddenly I didn't want to be quiet.

I didn't know adolescence was supposed to be like this. I had read books (serious ones, of course) about the physical changes I could expect, but I hadn't known I was capable of this sort of emotional turmoil. I felt dangerous. I don't mean that in a sexy way; I mean that I felt like a live grenade, unstable and explosive.

I clung to a few friends whom I felt sure were genuine and lashed out at them when they wanted their space. I didn't even know what I needed—a witness to my disintegration? One day I punched my friend Tom during art class, certain that he had become an enemy. Understand, these paranoid theories were not fully formulated. If they had been, I could have recognized them for the nonsense I had always disparaged. But the idea that my dad would eventually lose patience with me, would recognize how dangerous I had become and feel forced to take action, made perfect sense at the time. So one night I found myself out in the woods behind our house, having just run from a fight with my father that had ended with my hands around his throat.

I don't remember what the argument was about. I think I had forgotten it by the time I stood in those woods, staring at the back porch light. The lights of that house in the forest had meant specific things to the musicians on their road to Bremen: warmth and safety, food and shelter and companionship. But it must have meant the same things to the robbers.

Once we become adults it is tempting to reduce stories like "The Bremen Town Musicians" to symbols. A Marxist might read the robbers as captains of industry and the animals as the proletariat; a rock 'n' roll revisionist might see the clash between the Beatles and the pop music establishment or the Ramones versus disco. In life, though, such readings are suspect, and the nonsense I used to turn my nose up at is often a better reflection of the world as we experience it. For me the symbols that resonate most are the ones that are hardest to express without sounding trite.

That night was not the last time I argued with my father. It took me a long time to remember that he had given me stories and almost as long to realize that noise didn't have to rattle the windows to be a useful tool. But you have to be careful with it, or it can drive you out of your head.

I can't say that I understand the world any better now than I did when I was a child—the Muppets still seem pretty damn real to me—but I think I understand my father about as well as he understands me. Which is to say, imperfectly, but well enough to feel at home.

Vijay Seshadri

STORIES, REAL AND UNREAL

I.

My first exposure, or the first exposure I can remember, to the pleasures of narrative happened when I was a little over two years old, in Bangalore, in the second half of the 1950s. My father was in America, getting his PhD. My mother and I were living with my grandfather and his family in a house in the neighborhood known as Malleswaram. My grandmother had just died—the second- or third-earliest memory I have (the sequence of events is lost to me) is of making my way through a forest of adult legs to look into the room where she had been laid out on the floor, according to Indian custom, and was surrounded by her children, who sat in a semicircle and wailed and wept. My mother insists that I can't remember this, that I was too young, but I do, and remember many other things, too; the trauma of those weeks must have induced the birth of my consciousness. I remember the house was large, with mango and pomegranate trees and coconut palms in the garden and flowering bushes—hibiscus, I would guess—dotting the borders, with verandahs, broad teak doors (I didn't, of course, know then that they were teak), broad windows open to the subtropical breezes, and with a long driveway leading from the gate to the port-cochere at the main entrance. Sometimes a car, probably a Citroën but maybe an Indian-made Ambassador, would be parked there, its driver idling near it.

My grandfather was entitled to the car and driver because of his position in the administration of the state of Mysore, of which Bangalore was the most substantial city. He was the chief engineer of the state, and had reached a position eminent enough that it made the subsequent and rapid decline of his fortunes in the next decade even more shocking. His narrative is the one that dominates my mother's side of the family, and it has a tragic arc, given shape by the elements that often define tragedy—hubris, fate, in the form of my grandmother's death, in his own illness (he was a serious and heedless diabetic), and in the self-destructive rebellion of some of his children, and an incalculable, unforeseeable, and steep downward slide brought on by disastrous coincidences. It was anything but a fairy tale, and not just because it didn't have a happy ending. Unlike a fairy tale, it had no conclusion. Its morals were forever withheld; its meaning could never be resolved; nothing came full circle but, instead, trailed off into the enigmatic and incomprehensible. I sometimes think nothing is more important to my mother than finding a way of telling her father's story that will cause it to resolve. She tells it over and over again, to herself, to us, to whomever will listen, re-creating in helpless, frustrated, Balzacian detail—in order to find an escape hatch of narrative conclusiveness and thereby free herself—the early triumphs, the pride they engendered, the recklessness of the self-love, and the terrible fall, which she avoided witnessing by moving to America with my father after he received his degree and won a postdoctoral fellowship in Canada, and about which, for no reason I can see, since she was blameless and couldn't have imagined what would come, she feels unassuagable guilt.

Indians have a talent for grief. I remember a lot of crying going on in that house after my grandmother's death, weeks and weeks of it. Her many children would get together in little groups and talk and weep and weep again, or go off singly to weep in corners, on staircases, near the well in the garden. My babysitters were my teenage aunts, but because of their grief they were lax in watching over me. The house had a large interior courtyard, along one

side of which, near the entryway to the kitchen, there was a brazier of coals, over which, among other things, coffee beans were
roasted in a large, round-bottomed pan. I must have been left to
myself one day, and I decided it would be fun to run and jump
back and forth over the brazier, which had been left burning and
unattended. On one jump, I tripped and the coals scattered over
my bare legs, giving me extensive third-degree burns. (I had the
scars for a long time and I assumed that the discoloration of the
skin on my legs was permanent, but looking just now, while writing this, at my legs, I find that, finally, no trace of the scars remains
and the discoloration is entirely gone.)

I don't remember pain—the human body supposedly sup-
presses the memory of pain—but I do remember that I suddenly
became the center of attention. I was carried up by the ubiquitous
grief, both an object on which it could focus and a distraction from
it, and put in the bed my grandmother and grandfather once oc-
cupied (my grandfather wouldn't sleep in it anymore), a big four-
poster in the biggest bedroom of the house. The doctor came,
dressed my burns, and confined me to the bed for weeks. It was
there, in a blistering South Indian April, while recuperating under the mosquito netting, that I first heard the story of the birth of
Rama, incarnation of the divine principle, embodiment of kingly
and husbandly virtue, slayer of the demon Ravana. The three wives
of Darsaratha, king of Ayodhya, are barren. The king performs a
sacrifice to petition the gods for an heir to his throne. Out of the
sacrificial fire a divine messenger appears with a silver chalice full
of *paisa,* an ambrosial liquid pudding, which Indians consume to
this day, and which is made in our household of milk, sugar, car-
damom, saffron, and either vermicelli, poppy seed, or tapioca. The
king gives half the *paisa* to his first wife, Kausalya. She will be the
mother of Rama, avatar of Vishnu. To his second wife, Sumitra, he
gives half of what is left of the *paisa.* To his third wife, Kaikeyi,
he gives half of what remains (notice here the delicate hierarchi-
cal arithmetic at the heart of the domestic order of Indian kings),
who will give birth to Rama's brother Bharata. He bestows what

little is left over on Sumitra, who because of this extra bounty will give birth to twins—Lakshmana, Rama's shadow, and Shatrunga, bane of Rama's enemies.

2.

Do children like fairy tales? And, if children do like fairy tales, why do they like them? The answer to the first question has been deemed obvious by contemporary modern culture (even though it doesn't necessarily follow that because fairy tales often have children as main characters they were told and subsequently written down for children). Yes, children like fairy tales, and, moreover, as we know in the aftermath of Bruno Bettelheim, fairy tales have a value parents can approve of. They're therapeutic and allow children to process the dark materials of experience. Fairy tales are useful, for both children and adults. Which contains the answer to the second question. Children like fairy tales instinctively because they are an aid to cognition, they help them order the world around them. But is this actually the case? These assertions and explanations aren't far-fetched, but they aren't self-evident, either, and seen a certain way they look suspiciously reductive. Could we possibly know what a child likes and why, or what the intensity of his or her approval is? How, for example, would I have responded at the age of two to a Nathalie Sarraute novel? Or what sort of stories was I telling myself? It's hard to say.

But I know that I liked the story of Rama's birth not because of its fairy-tale qualities—the magical potion, the number three, etc.—or because it was an illumination of, or an antidote to, the grief floating around me but because of the *paisa*. I've been told that the entire Ramayana was recited to me while I was recuperating under the mosquito netting in the house in Malleswaram, but the *paisa* episode is the only one I can remember from that time, and it is still the only one in that vast and various epic which has resonance for me, and that was because of the *paisa* itself. *Paisa* was a dessert I loved throughout my childhood, and food is something a two-year-old understands. I can make a case, in fact, at least to myself, that all the fairy tales I liked—the ones I encountered in the English-language school run by Anglican nuns, where I was enrolled at three; in the elementary school in Ottawa, to which I was translated at the age of five; in the grade school I went to in Ohio—had something to do with eating. The wolf eats or gets eaten, the idiot girl (hasn't she figured it out yet?) eats the apple poisoned on one side, the birds eat the breadcrumb trail, the abandoned boy and girl eat the gingerbread house and will soon, if they don't watch out, be nicely cooked themselves, Goldilocks eats the porridge (a delicious word that made my mouth water when I was a kid). I dislike Hans Christian Andersen's stories almost as much for the fact that his characters rarely eat in them, and certainly never with gusto, as I do for the punitive and hideous Calvinism that secretly infects each sentence.

I was a good eater as a child, and had a capacity for taking things as they came. I didn't have a trace of sentimentality about my grandmother's death (older and more vulnerable to human beings, I did grieve for my grandfather twelve years later, though I had hardly known him). I was puzzled at my mother's behavior, but not overly. Big things were happening around me in those weeks of death, grief, and burns, and I had snapped to attention. It would be years before events made impressions on me as vivid as the events of those weeks did. Also, and this has stayed with me, I developed out of the different elements I was suddenly aware of, a precocious (to say the least) maturity about narrative, about stories and storytelling. I've read my share of fantasy fiction, but I have always taken greater pleasure in realism. I read Balzac all the time, and it would be nice to think that such a taste was vouchsafed to me in Bangalore when I was two. I enjoyed the story of Rama's birth. But even then, I like to think, I knew it was just a story, while all the other things happening around and to me were anything but.

Richard Siken

HANSEL

Why make a map? Why do anything at all? Not how, because hows are easy, series or sequence, one foot after the other, but existentially why bother, what does it solve? Well, if you don't need to, don't. Wouldn't that be great? Just don't make anything. The world is full of things already, the world is vast and wide and full of grace, and you will always be given the benefit of the doubt. Except that isn't true now, is it? Fact is, the world is full of things that are trying to kill you. We do not walk through a passive landscape. Sometimes you need a map to find the food, the hiding places.

I was a regular-style kid with a regular-style life. Things got bad, sure, but that was later. Grandma had stories about the war—running, hiding, privation—but that was later. I would discover that my father could speak German but refused to, was ashamed to—*We're Americans now*—but that was later. This is still the beginning, this is bedtime, early on. The window is over my bed and there are three trees outside the window, in the yard, the dark woods, well-framed and slowly moving in the breeze. Imagine that the world is made out of love. Now imagine that it isn't. Here is a story where everything goes wrong, here is a story where everyone has their back against the wall, here is a story where everyone is in pain and acting selfishly because if they don't, they'll die. Here is a story, not of good against evil, but of need against need against need, where everyone is at cross-purposes and everyone is to blame. How are you supposed to fall asleep to this?

Hard by a great forest lived a poor woodcutter who had come upon such hard times that he could no longer provide even daily bread for his wife and two children. "What is to become of us?" says the man. "Early tomorrow we will take the children into the thickest part of the forest and leave them there," says the woman. The two children, awake from hunger, heard everything their parents were saying. Trust no one. You are expendable. You are a burden. Why would you tell this to your child, who is about to go to sleep? *As soon as your eyes are shut, we will begin to plan your demise. If I were you, were smart, I'd stay awake, ever vigilant and terrified.* I would look out the window at those three trees and think about those two children. If you know the story, you know that Gretel saves the day, that women have power (mother, daughter, witch) and men (father and son) just flounder about. My father is telling me this story and I am an only child. There is no Gretel. He has no power. I am being warned and there is no out.

Gretel began to cry, but Hansel says, "Be quiet, don't worry. I know what to do." And with that he got up, pulled on his jacket, opened the lower door, and crept outside. *The lower door?* Fairy tales have rules. You are a princess or you aren't. You are pure at heart or you aren't. If you are pure at heart, or lucky, you might catch a break. And there are other rules, like: anything can happen. As well as: you will not get exactly what you want. Apples fall like raindrops, three drops of blood on snow can make a child, mirrors and birds can talk, but sometimes—as in "The Goose Girl"—when they kill your pony, you're supposed to feel blessed that he, the disembodied head, that is, can, thanks to the magic handkerchief, still give you good advice. I'm not suggesting the world is good, that life is easy, or that any of us are entitled to better. But please, isn't this the kind of thing you talk about in somber tones, in the afternoon, with some degree of hope and maybe even a handful of strategies? I think I'm getting mad now. Give me a second . . .

There's a lot to be said for humility and taking your lumps. Vanity, in a fairy tale, will make you evil. Vanity in the real world will

drive you nuts. Vanity makes you say things like "I deserved a better life than this." Which leads to entitlement issues, anxiety, de-
pression, an inability to approach the divine—out of frustration,
refusal, or blindness—and a shitty attitude. Maybe they should kill
your pony. *They?* I don't even know who they are. I wouldn't kill
your pony. I'd like to believe it, anyway. I'd like to believe I
wouldn't drag you out in to the woods and leave you there, either.
So far, it hasn't come up.

The lower door. Prolly a Dutch door, but I didn't know that
then, thought it was part of the magical anything goes dealio. Still
do. Even the most common nouns can take on an otherworldly
shine when lit improperly. The lower door, underground railroad,
a half-measure. Out he goes. The moon shines brightly and the
white pebbles in front of the house glisten like silver coins. Hansel
bends over and fills his jacket pockets with them, as many as will
fit. Then at daybreak, the woman comes and wakes the children.
"Get up, you lazybones. We are going into the woods to fetch
wood." She gives each one a piece of bread, saying, "Here is something for midday. Don't eat it any sooner, for you'll not get any
more." Gretel hides hers under her apron so she can carry his.
Hansel drops the pebbles from his pocket onto the path.

They arrive, middle of the woods, make a fire, rest. Because they
can hear the blows of an ax, they think that the father is nearby. It
is not an ax, it's a branch that he had tied to a dead tree and that
the wind was beating back and forth. After they had sat there a
long time, their eyes grow weary and they fall asleep. This is the
first iteration. They wake, it's dark, they cry, the moon rises, and
the pebbles shine, showing them the way. This is my favorite part.
It starts and ends here. The pebbles shine, the plan worked, Hansel
Triumphant. Lesson number one: Be sneaky and have a plan. But
the stupid boy goes back, makes the rest of the story postscript and
aftermath. He shouldn't have gone back. And this is the second lesson I took from the story: When someone is trying to ditch you,
kill you, never go back.

My father is reading me this story and sometimes it is just a
story and other times it is his story, his history, he is sharing a sad-

ness with me, an unfairness done to him that he cannot express, or it is the story of Exodus, or of World War II. My father creeps me out because he is telling me too many stories all at once and I do not believe that he is innocent, or pure at heart, and I want pebbles. I want a lower door. *They walked throughout the entire night, and as morning was breaking, they arrived at the father's house.* Stupid, stupid kids.

Second iteration: We must ditch the kids. The kids overhear. This time the lower door is locked. No pebbles. A forced march deeper into the woods and, bread in hand—*keep your hands where I can see 'em*—a trail of breadcrumbs. Sleeping, waking, crying, the moon rising, the crumbs gone. The narrator blames the birds. And you want to blame the birds as well. I blamed the birds for a long time. But in this story everyone is hungry, even the birds. And at this point in the story so many things have gone wrong, so many bad decisions made, that it's a wonder anyone would want to continue reading.

They walk all night, they walk all day, they eat a few berries, walk some more, and die. Yes, they die. They die as surely as the Little Match Girl dies, and this is not lost on me, even as a child. They die either because of the pebbles or from a lack of them. There is no way to win. Everyone is hungry, and the weak get tricked and do not survive. Or, they do. Which is lesson three: In language, the teller decides. A little house made out of bread with windows made of clear sugar. Sounds like they're dead. Sounds like the teller's gone crazy. In other fairy tales, the magic is there from the start. Here, starting so late in the story, it sounds like propaganda. *No, really, when I leave you for dead you'll find all the candy you could ever want. Hey little boy, wanna see the puppy in my windowless van?* And aside from the house, there's not much magic to this story. A witch who eats kids? Not magic, just another predator. She's hungry, the kids are hungry, the parents are hungry, the birds are hungry, the story's over now, it's just blather: a cage, a bone, an oven, a moment seized, discovered treasure, the journey home.

There are many definitions for poetry that are useful. I like "Poetry is language that does more than one thing" and "Poetry is the residue of a life lived." I use words like *pebbles,* like *residue. You are in terrible danger. Grab your pebbles and go. Make a trail away from doom and don't look back.* It works better than I thought it would. I also believe that anything can happen in words. The teller decides. I took it to heart. A spell, an incantation, a cake recipe. There is a bomb inside you. I can say that. It might be true. The Dalai Lama says we are born in bliss and Jesus says we are born in sin. I say, even if you do not believe in God, you must believe that we are born into narrative, one foot in front of the other, things happening after other things. And since you are always moving forward— pushed, pulled, or just strolling along—you might as well take note of how and where you're going. Many writers can point to an event in their lives where they gained permission to write. The story of Hansel (and Gretel) gave me a mandate to write, to describe the terrain, for myself as well as for anyone who might want to, need to, follow. There is something up ahead, in the distance, waiting for you like a mood or a room. Here is the brass key, this song, these poems I write, mouth-filler for hungers about to happen. You will come here, I can't stop that from happening, and they may even kill your pony, but I will be here, on the page, whispering to you. I have found the lower door and filled my jacket pocket with pebbles, as many as will fit. I am Hansel, your brother. I am Hansel, your partner. I am Hansel Triumphant, the father that you deserved.

Kieran Suckling

FROGS

> Sweet are the uses of adversity,
> Which like the toad, ugly and venomous,
> Wears yet a precious jewel in his head
> SHAKESPEARE

The suspect was "not your average maggot-looking dope dealer on the corner." At least that's what the police say. It was 1994, and he was arrested for possession of bufotenine, a Schedule 1 drug under the California Controlled Substances Act. The drug in question came in the form of four toads—Hanz, Franz, Peter, and Brian—that the suspect intended to smoke. Not the entire toad, but, as has been known to happen in fairy tales, its skin. More specifically, the parotid gland at the back of Hanz's head would be milked, dried, and smoked, causing our suspect to inform the police that he could "hear electrons jumping orbitals in his molecules."[1]

California outlawed bufotenine in 1970, but the toad smoker was the first to be arrested and charged under this law, probably because of a curious bufotenine panic in the early 1990s. News of hippie Australian toad lickers hit the U.S. press with the *Toronto News* screeching "Licking Toad a Dangerous New Craze," the *Guardian* proclaiming "It's Repulsive and Highly Dangerous," and

[1]. Information about the couple's case comes from *Modesto Bee*, "Toads Bring a New Look to Drug Bust," January 6, 1994; *Modesto Bee*, "Delay in Toad Case," March 2, 1994; *New York Times*, "Couple Avoids Jail in Toad Extract Case," May 1, 1994.

the *Los Angeles Times* warning that "Licking a Toad Is the Latest Way to Hallucinate."[2] A grave threat to America's future was at hand and state legislators took swift action. "They say these frogs grow to the size of a dinner plate," said Rep. Patrick Harris of South Carolina explaining his anti-bufotenine bill, "I don't want to see somebody walk across the Statehouse grounds with a frog on a leash and pick him up and lick him."[3] Indeed. State representative Beverly Langford warned Georgia legislators of "the extreme dangers of toad licking becoming the designer drug of choice in today's sophisticated society" and asked the state to determine if toad licking should be classed as a sex crime.[4] Both legislators were referring to the giant marine toad (*Bufo marinus*) whose natural range stretches from Texas through Mexico and Central America to the Amazon Basin of South America but was introduced in Florida, the Caribbean, Hawaii, the Philippines, and Australia. However, all of the more than two hundred species in the *Bufo* genus—including Europe's common toad (*Bufo vulgaris*) for which the compound was named—contain bufotenine. There isn't a pet shop in the United States and few ten-year-old boys that have not illegally possessed bufotenine.

The *Wall Street Journal* noted the arrest in a story bearing the headline "Toad-Smoking Gains on Toad-Licking among Drug Users," and indeed the arrest set off an unlikely war between adherents of licking and smoking. The latter asserted that bufotenine is unlikely to be psychoactive, and, if it is, the toxic effects, especially combined with the orally active bufotoxins and bufodienolides, would threaten the life and health of any would-be enthusi-

2. *The Guardian*, "Getting Their Kicks and Licks on the Toad to Rack and Ruin," July 11, 1990; *Toronto Star*, "Licking Toads a Dangerous New Craze," January 21, 1990; *Los Angeles Times*, "Toad Licking Leaves More than a Bad Taste in the Mouth," January 31, 1990.
3. Mitchell Landsberg, "Legislators Toady to Chickens, Marmots," *Los Angeles Times*, March 11, 1990
4. *The Guardian*, "Getting Their Kicks and Licks on the Toad to Rack and Ruin," July 11, 1990; Cox News Service, "His Story Has Warts in It," February 14, 1990.

ast long before a potential ecstatic state would set in.[5] They pro-
mote another compound, 5-methoxy-N,N-dimethyltryptamine (5-
MEO-DMT) as a more compelling hallucinogen. 5-MEO-DMT is
present in only the Sonoran Desert toad (*Bufo alvarius*), is active
only if smoked, and the smoking eliminates other toxic compounds. Scientists believe 5-MEO-DMT is one of the most powerful hallucinogens found in nature and perhaps the only hallucinogen present in an animal. Hanz, Franz, Peter, and Brian were
Sonoran Desert toads and clearly destined for the pipe.

The lickers point out that while the Sonoran Desert toad's range
extends only from southeastern California to southwestern New
Mexico and south to Sinaloa, archaeological artifacts, linguistic associations, and folk stories from around the world suggest a hallucinogenic use of toads and toadstools. Though the Sonoran
Desert toad inspired the Arizona-based Church of the Toad of
Light, and may have been traded by Native Americans into parts
of Central and South America (though physical evidence is lacking), it cannot explain the consistent worldwide association of
toads and transformative/psychedelic experiences, from Mayan
burial rituals to the Temple at Delphi, Chinese ch'an su medicine,
and European frog prince stories.

Scientific research, which has primarily been carried out on
murderers, schizophrenics, and LSD-addicted rats, has not been
terribly helpful. The rats showed some proclivity to press a button
marked "LSD" when given bufotenine, but the results were not
statistically significant. The murderers and schizophrenics, busy
with nausea, retching, vomiting, nystagamus, and their skin's turning "the color of eggplant," pressed no LSD buttons. One nearly
drowned in her own saliva, another had to be resuscitated. Nasty
stuff, but they undoubtedly experienced hallucinogenic sights and

5. See T. Lyttle, D. Goldstein, and J. J. Gartz, "Bufo Toads and Bufotenine: Fact and
Fiction Surrounding an Alleged Psychedelic," *Journal of Psychoactive Drugs* 28, no.
3 (1996): 267–90; Wade Davis and Andrew T. Weil, "Identity of a New World Psychoactive Toad," *Ancient Mesoamerica* 3 (1992): 51–59; and Davis, *Shadows in the
Sun*.

visions. One subject confessed: "Words can't come. My mind feels crowded. When I start on a thought, another one comes along and clashes with it. . . . I am here and not here." Another recovered a suppressed memory from age three of seeing her mother dying of a uterine hemorrhage. More recently, self-experimenters have demonstrated hallucinogenic bufotenine effects in carefully controlled environments.[6]

Whether the California legislature was mistaken in outlawing bufotenine, our suspect was the first person prosecuted for toad frolicking since Maria de Illara in 1611.[7] De Illara, a sixty-nine-year-old Basque woman, confessed that the devil had instructed her to pound up toads in water and rub the ointment upon her chest down to her navel and in her armpits to obtain the power of flight. Flying ointments were well known in Europe and typically included plants in the nightshade family, especially henbane, jimson weed, belladonna, and mandrake. They contain atropine and scopolamine (6,7-epoxytropine tropate), powerful but deadly hallucinogens. They often included mashed toad as well. Dosage is critical to survival and difficult to control orally, so the ointment was sometimes placed on the end of stick or the handle of a broom or pitchfork and then inserted into the vagina, giving rise to the image of witches flying on broomsticks.[8]

The first toad trial, which was also the first witch trial in England, took place in 1566.[9] Elizabeth Francis received from her grandmother a toad that, through dark contrivance, had been

6. See J. Ott, "Pharmanopo-psychonautics: Human Intranasal, Sublingual, Intrarectal, Pulmonary and oral Pharmacology of Bufotenine," *Journal of Psychoactive Drugs* 33, no. 3 (2001): 273–81; and Alexander T. Shulgin and Ann Shulgin, *Tihkal: The Continuation* (Berkeley, Calif.: Transform Press, 1997).

7. Adrian Morgan, *Toads and Toadstools: The Natural History, Folklore, and Cultural Oddities of a Strange Association* (Berkeley, Calif.: Celestial Arts, 1995).

8. Ibid.; Andrew Sherratt, "Flying up with the Souls of the Dead," *British Archaeology* 15, June 1996.

9. Willyam Powell, "The examination and confession of certaine Wytches at Chensforde in the Countie of Essex before the Quenes majesties Judges, the XXVI daye of July Anno 1566," in Marion Gibson, *Early Modern Witches: Witchcraft Cases in Contemporary Writing* (London: Routledge, 2000).

transformed into a cat named Sathan. It could be compelled "by pricking her hand or face and putting the blood in his mouth which he sucked." Applying toad secretions to a wound was and is a method of bufotenine ingestion.[10]

With a blood offering/cat-bufotenine ingestion, Elizabeth bade Sathan to bewitch a certain Andrew Byles. Sathan agreed but stipulated that Byles should "abuse" her before marriage. The deal was struck, the abuse rendered, but Byles refused to marry. Sathan killed him, then counseled Elizabeth on the use of an herbal abortive, probably ergot, another dangerous hallucinogen. Compelled again, Sathan bewitched Christopher Francis to marriage. It didn't end well. The official record tells us that the couple "lived not so quietly as she desyred, beinge stirred to much unquietnes and moved to swearing and cursinge." At Elizabeth's bidding, Sathan killed their infant daughter, turned himself into a toad, and hid in Christopher's shoe. Upon touching the not-so-hapless toad with his toe, Christopher became incurably lame.

Elizabeth traded Sathan to Agnes Waterhouse for a sweet cake. Mother Waterhouse was, unfortunately, prone to neighborly quarrels and in short time bade Sathan to drown one neighbor's cow and another's geese. Hogs were similarly dispatched and butter curds made to be lost. She was generous to Sathan, however, for in each instance he was given not only a drop of blood but a whole chicken that "he ate up clean . . . and she could find remaining neither bones nor feathers."

Confessing to two murders and a hobbling, Elizabeth Francis was sentenced to two years in jail.[11] Agnes Waterhouse denied being a witch but admitted to conspiring with Sathan against live-

---

10. Morgan, *Toads and Toadstools*.

11. Five years after being released from prison, Elizabeth Francis was again found guilty of witchcraft. Though England had a two-strikes-you're-out witchcraft policy, she was mysteriously sentenced to only a year in jail. Six years after she was released, she stood trial for witchcraft yet again and this time was sentenced to death. See "A Detection of damnable driftes, practized by three Witches arraigned at Chelmisforde in Essex, at the laste Assises there holden, which were executed in Aprill 1579" in Gibson, *Early Modern Witches*.

stock and curds. She was hanged by the neck on July 29, 1566. Though it was not unheard of for medieval Europeans to put animals on trial, this was not Sathan's fate. Upon hearing the Lord's Prayer in Latin, he reverted to a toad and hopped away.

Bewitching, toads, and marriage continue to intersect in modern tellings of the "Frog Prince" and some versions of "Beauty and the Beast." The stories play out very differently in the United States and Europe. Although I don't disagree that an excessive and narrow morality has simplified and sanitized the American versions,[12] it's worth noting that this critique has largely been developed from an anthropocentric perspective that deprives the frog of biological properties and the ability to actively participate in the human drama. The frog is reduced to a symbol. Such thoroughgoing and naive humanism would have been inconceivable to the early tellers of these tales. A pharmacological—or better, ecological—perspective adds depth to the stories and their evolution.

A petulant princess drops a golden ball down a well. A frog offers to retrieve it but only if the princess promises to let him be her companion, to dine at her table, to sleep in her bed. She falsely agrees, takes the ball, and runs back to her castle, leaving the frog behind. The frog eventually makes his way to the castle, where the king forces the disgusted princess to keep her promise. In a German version she grabs the frog as it tries to enter her bed and smashes him against the wall screaming, "Now you'll get your rest, you disgusting frog!" The violent act breaks an evil spell unknown to the princess, transforming the frog into his original form, a handsome prince. In a British version she beheads the frog. In a Polish version the frog is replaced by a snake, which is cut in two. A Lithuanian version has her burn the snake's skin. A Russian "Beauty and the Beast" story reverses the genders and has the

12. See E. W. Harries, "The Violence of the Lambs," *Marvels & Tales: Journal of Fairy-Tale Studies* 19, no. 1 (2005): 54–66, and Don Haase, "German Fairy Tales and America's Cultural Wars: From Grimm's *Kinder-und Hausmarchen* to William Bennett's *Book of Virtues*," *German Politics and Society* 13 (Fall 1995): 17–25.

prince burn the female toad's skin. In American versions the princess places him on her pillow or compassionately kisses him.

So we're back to lickers versus smokers (and perhaps cutters). In either case, while the stories have irreducible gender, father-daughter, and marriage themes, they also have an irreducible ecological theme. Animals become human and humans become animal. The transformation/insight is not accomplished by word magic but by kissing, licking, smoking, ingesting, and even appreciating the other. Bufotenine, like other powerful compounds, can cross the species boundary because it is an analog to human serotonin. It and the human brain are structured and biologically destined to interact.

But the possibility of interacting is becoming increasingly remote, even impossible. The Sonoran Desert toad is an endangered species in California. It's been extirpated from the state since the 1970s. Toad smoker got his from Arizona. The human experience of the species has gone extinct for most Californians. Tuolumne County, where the arrest occurred, is home to the California red-legged frog, made famous by Mark Twain as the Celebrated Frog of Calaveras County. Once abundant enough to support eighty thousand diners a year in San Francisco, it was placed on the federal endangered species list in 1996. There will be no more licking or eating, and very little seeing or hearing, of the California red-legged frog. It was long ago replaced at jumping frog contests by exotic bullfrogs. A third Calaveras resident, the foothill yellow-legged frog, is in the process of being placed on the endangered list.

"Beauty and the Beast" stories changed dramatically in the twentieth century, focusing less on the beauty's redeeming and civilizing of the beast and more on the beast's animal dignity and struggle to survive.[13] This should come as no surprise. Fairy tales

---

13. Marina Warner, "Go Be a Beast: Beauty and the Beast II," in *From the Beast to the Blonde: On Fairy Tales and Their Tellers* (New York: Farrar, Straus and Giroux, 1994). In Jon Scieszka's *The Frog Prince Continued,* the unhappily married couple kisses again and both people happily turn into frogs.

evolve to communicate the existential situation of the communities that tell them. That situation is less a matter of received values and beliefs than it is an engagement with the real. In our world, where the plant and animal foundations of our symbols and metaphors are increasingly threatened with extinction and the assumptions of humanism appear increasingly barren, fairy tales cannot but reexamine the human-animal relation.

Jeff VanderMeer

THE THIRD BEAR

I. Masha and the Bear

The first bear may be uncouth, but not unkind, despite appearances. His English isn't good and he lives alone in a cottage in the forest, but no one can say he doesn't try. If he didn't try, if the idea of trying, and thus of restraint, were alien to him, the first bear wouldn't live in a cottage at all. He'd live in the deep forest and all anyone would see of him, before the end, would be hard eyes and the dark barrel of his muzzle. The third bear would be so much in him that no first bear would be left.

The first bear is a man's man, or, rather, a bear's bear: "golden brown, with enormous claws on his padded feet and sharp, pure-white fangs bigger than a person's hands, and eyes a startling blue." This bear smells like mint and blueberries, and his name is Bear.

One day a girl named Masha gets lost in the woods. Bear finds her and takes her back to his cottage. He refuses to show her the way home, for his cottage is a mess and, as I may have mentioned, so is his English. Masha can help him with both disasters, although she isn't happy about the situation. She thinks Bear is the creature her parents warned her about when they told her not to go into the forest. But Bear is the first bear, not the third bear. In an odd way Bear has saved her from the third bear.

Of course, Masha doesn't see it that way—and why should she? It's largely a matter of degree and not just because she can't imagine what worse might happen to her. Bear is gruff with Masha,

166 · JEFF VANDERMEER

makes her work long hours, and ignores her pleas to be shown the way back to her village. As far as Masha's concerned, this is as bad as it gets.

This dynamic continues for awhile, with Masha afraid to run off blindly while Bear's not looking. But then an odd thing begins to happen to Bear: the longer he talks to Masha and grows fond of her company, his English improving every week, he begins to feel bad for her. He begins to understand how lost, alone, and cut off she feels—in part because he feels the same way. Still, Bear enjoys the captive audience so much he does not allow his concern for her well-being to override his need for companionship. He cannot bring himself to show Masha the way home, for surely that means he will lose her forever.

One day Masha finds a huge, bear-sized basket under a pile of Bear's dirty clothes, and she has an idea.

She bakes some pies and tells Bear, "You need to let me go back to my village. I want to take my parents some pies to eat. I promise I'll come back. Just show me the way."

Bear just laughs and says, "Naw. That not happening. Who would clean all day? This place is mess."

Masha begins to cry, and this is more than Bear can, well, bear.

There's no real reason for him to do as Masha requests except that he cares for her. She's given him a way to help her without having to take the initiative, to be seen, somehow, as weak or vulnerable. Sometimes that's all any of us needs.

"Okay," Bear says. "I take pies to parents. But you stay here."

Masha smiles through her tears and says, "I will, Bear. I will! But I'm going to climb that tall tree outside of your cottage to keep an eye on you. I don't want you eating any of those pies along the way!"

Fine, says Bear, and when he lurches off for a few minutes to scratch his back against a pine tree, Masha hides herself in the picnic basket. Bear picks it up and off he goes, in his plodding, head-swaying bear way.

Every so often Bear stops and, tempted, begins to open the picnic basket. Each time Masha, supposedly seeing him from the top of a pine tree, shouts, "Remember, Bear—those pies are for my parents! Don't eat them!" Each time, Bear, caught, sighs and continues on without opening the basket.

Or, rather, that's the traditional version. In the original version too, Bear's English is fine from the beginning of the story. And not much of anything is revealed about Bear's internal reaction to Masha's pie delivery request.

But I didn't like the traditional version very much when I read it. I mean, I loved the description of Bear and the dynamic between Bear and Masha, but the picnic basket didn't make any sense. How dumb does Bear have to be to not know that Masha is in the basket?

No, Bear had to be in the know for any of that to work. In real life, in my version, Bear knows very well that Masha is in the basket. He's still a real bear, even if he's been anthropomorphized a bit. He can smell that Masha's in the basket. As for a bear's hearing and Masha's pathetic attempts to throw her voice, the less said the better—except that her attempts probably endear her to him all the more.

So:

"I see you!" Masha says. "I see you from my tree! Don't eat any of those pies!"

Bear grins a toothy grin. "Uh-oh," he says loudly. "Masha must see me from the tall tree. I guess not eat pie."

In the original version, when Bear gets to the village, Masha's parents mistake Bear for the third bear they're always warning their daughter about and chase him away with a shotgun. Bear drops the basket and out jumps Masha, safe and sound. Although the folktale doesn't tell us any more about what happens to Bear, I guess he must go back to his messy cottage, sad and lonely and embittered. Maybe one day, lacklorn, he wanders into the deep forest, encounters the third bear, and that's that.

I like Masha better than Bear in this folktale, even though I feel affection for Bear because I recognize in him attributes of myself and my fellow males. After all, folktales have an odd way of stylizing violence and horrible actions by stripping them of their three-dimensional detail. In a sense, they sometimes function like those cartoons in which the mouse hits the cat with a hammer. If it happened in real life, you'd recoil in horror.

Bear is perfectly cute in his role as shambling, inconsiderate ursine. Despite this, at base Bear is a kidnapper who makes Masha into his work slave, no matter what his motivations. It is very nearly the stereotype of the unequal marriage or the unequal relationship in our culture. Most men have played the role of that bear at some time or another—the guy who doesn't want to appear weak, who needs a civilizing influence, who at heart is actually somewhat vulnerable and just needs someone to care about for that to come to the fore. Because, let's face it, Masha isn't Bear's daughter in this folktale. She's not quite his wife either, thank god, but close enough.

Now, do you want to know what *really* happens to Bear? And what *really* happened at the end of the folktale?

In the *true* version that no one wants to talk about, Bear reaches the village at dusk, when he's able to walk down the streets without fear of discovery.

> Soon, he came to Masha's parents' house. He set the basket down and knocked on the door.
>
> Slowly, Masha's father opened the door and stared up at the great bear.
>
> "Who are you?" Masha's father asked. He didn't sound frightened, probably because Masha's mother was hidden behind the door holding a loaded shotgun.
>
> "I'm Bear," said Bear. "And I bring your daughter home, and pies. She's in basket right there. All in return is you help me more with English."

The parents accept Bear's proposal once they see their daughter is unharmed. Bear becomes civilized and never returns to the forest. He even runs for mayor. Masha, meanwhile, grows up to become a smart, talented woman who forgives Bear and even becomes his friend—and definitely never gets lost in the forest again.

Bear never gets lost in the woods again either. That third bear frightens him so much that sometimes his nightmares make it hard for him to breathe.

II. The Farmer's Cat

The second bear isn't any tidier than the first. It's not that he's messy—it's that he carries his mess in his context. For many years the second bear, whose name is Bear, doesn't realize he's a bear. He doesn't even think he's a cat. He thinks he's a human being. So there's the mess in his context, peeking out.

What am I talking about?

The second bear—Bear—inhabits a trickster tale involving a farmer and trolls. Every winter the trolls smash down the door to the farmer's house and make themselves at home for a month. They eat all of his food, drink all of the water from his well, guzzle down all of his milk, break his furniture, and fart whenever they feel like it. Their leader, Mobhead, is a monstrous troll with an enormous head. It is so large that it has to be propped up with a head crutch.

The farmer has no choice but to let them trash his farm every year. Until one autumn a traveling merchant comes by, selling orphaned bear cubs. An idea forms in the farmer's head.

The next year, when the trolls come barreling through, they find the new cat.

One of the other trolls—a deformed troll, with a third eye protruding like a tube from its forehead—prodded the ball of fur with one of its big clawed toes. "It's a cat, I think. Just like the last one. Another juicy, lovely cat."

A third troll said, "Save it for later. We've got plenty of time."

The farmer, who had been watching all this, said to the trolls, "Yes, this is our new cat. But I'd ask that you not eat him. I need him around to catch mice in the summer, or, when you come back next time, I won't have any grain, and no grain means no beer."

The misshapen troll sneered. "A pretty speech, farmer. But don't worry about the mice. We'll eat them all before we leave."

But the farmer gets Mobhead to swear to leave the cat alone. And Mobhead agrees, smug and secure in the omniscience of his enormous skull.

Now, in the original version of this tale, the leader of the trolls doesn't have an enormous head—this is pure extrapolation on my part because I like the idea of head crutches—but the trolls are all such knuckleheads that the idea of their mistaking a bear cub for a kitten isn't that outlandish. The idea of their leader acquiescing to the farmer's request seemed slightly more outlandish. In my version of the tale Mobhead grants the request but says:

> Hmmm. I must admit I've grown fond of you, farmer, in the way a wolf is fond of a lamb. And I do want our winter resort to be in good order next time we come charging down out of the frozen north. Therefore, *although I have this nagging feeling I might regret this,* I will let you keep the cat. But everything else we're going to eat, drink, ruin, or fart on. I just want to make that clear.

Some characters in folktales just have a set role to play, regardless of logic or giant heads. A few of these characters, over time, develop a self-awareness about that role. However, that doesn't mean they can ever escape it.

At this point in the folktale, I stopped reading for a while and I started thinking about that ball of fur curled up in the basket, the second bear, known as Bear. Here is an orphan that has never known its mother. Here is a bear sold to be a cat. Does the farmer raise Bear as a cat? Does the farmer raise Bear as a bear and just present him to the trolls as a cat? Exactly what sense of identity does Bear have at this point?

The farmer's a sly character in the original folktale. The trolls are colorful and profane. But Bear is the interesting one because Bear has to perform multiple roles. The second bear is a kind of consummate actor—consummate because he doesn't even know he's an actor.

Because it's pretty clear to me that, even if it's never stated in the folktale, the farmer raises Bear as if he were a human being with a bit of the third bear in him.

So, what happens next?

Two years later, the trolls come by and the farmer's "cat" is all grown up: "There rose a huge shadow with large yellow eyes and rippling muscles under a thick brown pelt. The claws on the shadow were big as carving knives, and the fangs almost as large." Bear savages the trolls, just like a bear.

> Suddenly they heard a growl that turned their blood to ice and set them to gibbering, and at their rear there came the sound of bones being crunched, and as they turned to look and see what was happening, they were met by the sight of some of their friends being hurled at them with great force.

Mobhead is furious with the farmer, but Bear is too much for the trolls. They won't be coming back.

In the traditional version from Norway, that's the end of the story: the farmer triumphant, the trolls vanquished. All is right in the world again. It is the classic trickster tale—one that often presupposes the stupidity of the opposition, unfortunately, a kind of brain-versus-brawn equation that allows for none of the clever complexity of, say, Roadrunner versus Coyote or Holmes versus Moriarty. And, again, we don't find out what happens to Bear afterward. These bears are always falling off the map.

But when I finished reading, I was still thinking about Bear and his role in the story. If you look at it from Bear's perspective, what a screwed-up childhood! He's orphaned. He's sold into the farmer's family under false pretenses. The farmer makes him part of the busy yet stable farm life—"The farmer and his cat would take long walks through the fields, the farmer teaching the cat as much about the farm as possible. And he believed that the cat even appreciated some of it"—but the farmer also has to be a cold-blooded troll killer when it comes right down to it.

The untold story within this folktale is about our place in the world. Where do we fit in? How much are we shaped by our environment, how much by our heritage? The farmer knows who he is, as do the trolls. They're more boring for it, but I'm sure Bear would prefer to be boring rather than unsettled and confused, the reader's boredom level rarely a concern of fictional characters. Bear is, in a sense, the classic teenager—neither fish nor fowl, capable of restraint and unbridled passion in almost the same instant.

So how does this folktale *really* end? How can it end, except with uncertainty?

Once inside, the farmer and the bear laughed.

"Thanks, Mob-Eater," the farmer said. "You looked really fierce."

The bear huffed a deep bear belly laugh, sitting back on its haunches in a huge comfy chair the farmer had made for him.

"I am really fierce, father," the bear said. "But you should have let me chase them. I don't like the taste of troll all that much, but, oh, I do love to chase them."

"Maybe next year," the farmer said. "Maybe next year. But for now, we have chores to do. I need to teach you to milk the cows, for one thing."

"But I hate to milk the cows," the bear said. "You know that."

"Yes, but you still need to know how to do it, son."

"Very well. If you say so."

They waited for a few minutes until the trolls were out of sight, and then they went outside and started doing the farm chores for the day.

Soon, the farmer thought, his wife and children would come home, and everything would be as it was before. Except that now they had a huge talking bear living in their house.

Sometimes folktales didn't end quite the way you thought they would. But they *did* end.

At least, this is the way *I* think the folktale should end. With Bear blithely unaware of the contradiction between third-bear blood-thirstiness and human boy frustration with chores. With the farmer realizing that the solution to one problem may have created another, altogether more deadly and personal, problem.

Because, ultimately, the second bear is still a wild animal, not a human being at all.

III. The Third Bear

The third bear is problematic. It doesn't think of itself as a bear. It doesn't want to be in this essay. The third bear is always waiting to be written. He lives in the deepest of deep forest. He has no patience with human folktales. He lives rough and is all animal. No taint of human in this bear. He has no name, not even "Bear." He does sometimes exist at the edges of other folktales that are not about him at all—spoor dropping in the dark part of the woods; the sense of menace that forms the backdrop to some more brightly lit tale. You can just see him in the dark recesses of the foliage in the paintings of Rousseau. This is the bear that Masha's parents warned her about. This is the bear that existed in the crunch of bone and spurt of blood when the second bear was slaughtering trolls.

But this is an essay about folktales, so let me put the third bear in that context.

Once upon a time . . .
One terrible stormy night . . .
There once was a . . .
Three bears once . . .

Once there lived a creature that might have been a bear. This "bear" came to the forest near the village, and soon anyone who used the forest trail, day or night, disappeared, carried off to the creature's lair. By the time even large convoys went through the forest, they would discover two or three of their number missing.

A straggling horseman, his mount cantering along, just blood-stains and bits of skin sticking to the saddle. A cobbler gone but for a blood-soaked hat.

The villagers were distraught. If they didn't use the trail through the forest, they couldn't bring in food from the farmers on the other side. Without that trail they couldn't bring their goods to market. They were stuck in a nightmare.

Slowly they realized that they couldn't wait for the third bear to devour them all. They had to strike back.

The village's strongest man, Clem, a blacksmith, volunteered to fight the beast. He had arms like most people's thighs. His skin was tough from years of being exposed to flame. With his full black beard he almost looked like a bear himself.

"I'll go, and I'll go willingly," he told the village elders. "I've not met the beast I couldn't best. I'll squeeze the *a* out of him." And he laughed, for he had a passable sense of humor, although the village elders chose to ignore it.

Fitted in chain mail and leather armor, carrying an old sword some knight had once left by mistake in the village, Clem set forth in search of the third bear.

He left the path almost immediately, wandered through the underbrush to the heart of the forest, where the trees grew so black and thick that the only glimmer of light came reflected from water glistening on leaves. The smell in that place carried a hint of offal, so he figured he was close.

Clem had spent so much time beating things into shape that he had not developed a sense of fear, for he had never been beaten. But the smell in his nostrils did make him uneasy.

Clutching his sword, he came upon a hill and a cave inside. From within the cave a green flame beckoned.

A lesser man might have turned back, but not Clem. He didn't have the sense God gave a donkey. Into the cave he went.

Inside he found the third bear. And behind the third bear, arranged around the walls of the cave, the heads of the third bear's victims. The heads had been painstakingly painted and mounted on stands. They were all in various states of decay.

Many bodies lay stacked neatly in the back of the cave. Some had been mutilated. All had been defiled in some way. The wavery green light came from a candle the third bear had placed in the back of the cave to display his handiwork. The smell was so horrible, Clem had to put a hand over his mouth. And as he took it all in, the methodical nature of it, the fact that the third bear had, in fact, eaten only a few of his victims, he found something inside of him tearing and then breaking.

"I . . . ," he said and looked into the eyes of the third bear. "I . . ."

Clem stood there, frozen, as the third bear disemboweled him and tore his head from his shoulders.

The third bear had no use for heroes. Except, possibly, as part of a pattern of heads.

A month later Clem's head was found on the trail in the forest. Apparently, it hadn't fit the pattern. By then, four or five more people had been killed, one on the outskirts of the village. The situation had become desperate. Several villagers had risked leaving, and some had even made it through. But fear kept most in the village, locked into a kind of desperate fatalism that made their eyes hollow as they stared into some unknowable distance.

Over time, the village sent four or five of its strongest and most clever men and women to fight the third bear.

One, before the end, said to the third bear, "I think you were misunderstood as a child."

Another said, before fear clotted her windpipe, "You just need love."

A third, even as he watched his intestines slide out of his body, said, "Surely there is something we can do to appease you?"

The third bear said nothing. He had no snappy comebacks. No pithy sayings. No wisdom. His conversation was through his work, and he said what he wanted to say very eloquently in that regard.

The villagers became ritualistic and primitive and listless. They feared the forest so much that they ate berries and branches at the outskirts of their homes and never hunted wild game. Their skin became ever more pale and they stopped washing themselves. They believed the words of madmen and adopted strange customs. They stopped wearing clothes. They would defecate in the street. At some point they lost sight of reason entirely and sacrificed virgins to the third bear. They took to mutilating their bodies, thinking that this is what the third bear wanted them to do. Some few in whom reason persisted had to be held down and mutilated by others. A few, during the winter, cannibalized those who froze to death, and others who had not died almost wished they had.

By the time the third bear finished his pattern and moved on, the remaining villagers had all become no different than he.

And they all lived happily ever after.

There are always curious eyes peering out from the forest in a certain kind of folktale. Something hidden in the middle distance. Readers often think they are wolf eyes. But they are not the eyes of wolves. They are the eyes of the third bear. Peering from darkness into darkness.

The original folktales often served as literal warnings against wolves, bears, and other threats prevalent in a preindustrial world. When folktales became civilized, they developed more refined subtexts about human predators or dangerous situations. They began to impart advice, in a sense, that had to be extracted from that subtext. We've become quite adroit at infusing and extracting this subtext as writers and readers. We add postmodern twists to our folktales—updating them for what we feel the modern world needs from them. In the process sometimes, ironically enough, we make them more distant and less visceral than they need to be to work for us in the modern world.

But the smell of the third bear gives him away. It's the smell of piss and blood and shit and bubbles of saliva and of half-eaten food. It's what we forget is always with us no matter now big our cities get, how advanced our civilization. To say the third bear is all bear is to miss the point. To say that the third bear needs no symbolism but is simply himself is also to miss the point.

Sometimes I think modern fairy tales should be horror tales, that to encompass all the ferocity and animal intensity at the core of the past century's excesses, we need a little bit of the third bear in everything we write.

But, at the very least, when we reinvent our folktales, we need to acknowledge the third bear, even if only by his absence.

Sometimes the author has no recourse. Sometimes there is nothing I can do.

Willy Vlautin

THE BOY WHO COULD NOT BE SCARED

My grandparents lived within a mile of the ocean, and in the summer I'd stay with them. In the mornings my grandmother and I would walk down to the beach, to the edge of the water, and she'd lay down a towel and sit there for hours and watch me swim. When I'd take a break she'd give me money and I'd run up to the food stand they had there, and I'd order us lunch and bring it back to her.

She was a great old lady. She was the kindest person I knew. She was a really plain and humble woman. She was also very shy and had bad nerves, and even as a kid I knew I had bad nerves and I've always been shy. As a kid, being with her was easy; it was the nearest to heaven I've ever been.

In the afternoon we'd walk back to her house and play cards. In the evening she'd read to me. Sometimes novels, sometimes fairy tales. She had a great reading voice. She'd been an English teacher for years. *Johnny Tremain* was a favorite of mine. She read it to me countless times. Another favorite was a book of Grimms' fairy tales, in particular, "The Story of the Youth Who Went Forth to Learn What Fear Was." From the first go-through I was in love with the story.

He was half the kid I was and half the kid I wanted to be.

My brother was just like his brother. My brother fit in with the family; he was good-looking and an A student. He was outgoing. He had girlfriends. He'd sit around the fireplace at my dad's house and play guitar for my dad's wife and her family. My mother adored him, and my father was proud of him.

Me, I had the bad nerves and was shy and didn't talk.

I could disappear in a room full of people or disappear at the dinner table with just the three of us sitting there. My mom, my brother, and me. I didn't mind it. I liked it like that. Disappearing was a relief.

My mom had bad nerves, but I didn't know that until years later. Yet even when I was a kid my grandmother knew about me and I knew about her. We had our pact that way. She understood my bad nerves, and she treated me with nothing but kindness and gentleness.

And me, I treated and thought of her as a saint.

Whenever I'd say to her, "Could you read the one about the boy who can't be scared," she'd always find the book and read it. And that's how that boy became a hero to me.

The boy who couldn't be scared was strong and honest and proud. No one understood him, and this caused him as much pain in the fairy tale as it did me in my own life. And no one would help him either. He had no support or love in his home. He wanted more than anything to fit in. His problem was that he feared nothing, and he thought if he could learn fear he'd fit in, that he'd find his way.

I remember from the story that his frustrated father thought him foolish and a bit deranged.

So in the story, the father hands him off to a sexton who promises to put fear into the boy. The boy, however, shocks the sexton and stands up for himself. He isn't scared of the man. The sexton tells the father the boy has the devil in him and that there's nothing he can do to save the boy. Of course, the father believes the man and ostracizes his son. He gives the boy a little money and tells him to head out into the world. He says, "Go into the wide world, and tell no one from whence you come, and who is your father, for I have reason to be ashamed of you." The father washes his hands of his son, so the boy is forced to set out alone to try and find fear, hoping that by doing so he'll fit in, that finally he'll belong. That maybe once he can shudder, he'll be able to go home.

That's a line that always got me, that part about the shudder and going home.

So the boy is directed to the haunted castle and is told by the king that he will learn to fear there. Inside the old castle he faces the two huge black devilish cats, legions of dogs, a group of evil men, and yet nothing scares him. He faces down the haunted castle and chases away the darkness in it. In doing so the boy receives riches beyond his wildest dreams, and he gets to marry the daughter of the king. He becomes respected, and he becomes royalty.

Most of all, he falls deeply in love with his new wife, and for the first time in his life he is accepted and loved.

Yet the boy still does not understand fear. It troubles him greatly that he can't understand fear, and he tells his wife this over and over. This frustrates her to the point she empties a bucket of cold water and gudgeons over him while he sleeps (I didn't know what gudgeons were, and so this detail seemed especially important and mysterious to me). The boy wakes in fear, he begins to shudder, and here the story ends.

As a kid I didn't understand the ending of this fairy tale at all. I mean, I was just glad the boy fell in love and became a wealthy prince. He was the misunderstood kid that no one likes who gets the money and the girl. It doesn't get much better than that. His final understanding of what it means to *shudder* went over my head.

I remember asking my grandmother what it meant and why he was "finally scared." Why would the evil cats and dogs and his cousin in the coffin not scare him, but a bucket of water and minnows would?

Every time she read me this story, I'd ask her that question, again and again, like the boy in the story who keeps telling his wife he can't understand fear. "I don't understand the ending," I'd tell my nice grandmother. She was always so patient with me.

Because, my grandmother told me, because he had found love. He loved his wife greatly, and she accepted him, and she loved him back. It was the first time he'd experienced love. There had been no love in his home from his father or brother. It was his wife whom he loved and felt love from. Out of frustration his wife decided to show him fear, decided to scare him.

Because he gets scared, he becomes human. Because, my grandmother said, love makes you human. And the loss of love is pain, is fear, and is sadness. The boy's wife had hurt him. Before he had nothing to lose, and now, of course, he did.

He had never felt love so he never knew what it was like to shudder, my grandmother told me in her patient tone. She was such a nice old lady, like I said before. I felt really safe with her, and she never minded all of the questions I asked over and over again. "Why does he shudder? Why does he shudder?"

The tale always stuck with me, and as the years passed my grandmother and I stayed close. We would write each other, and I'd call her more than I would call anyone else I knew. She was the only person in my family who I ever told I loved. I would end all of my calls that way, all of my postcards and letters, telling her I loved her. It might not sound like much, but for me it was. It was the only time I really used that word.

I grew up a scared kid. Everything kept me up at night. But the thought of my grandmother could calm me down. And I'll always remember her telling me about that kid who was scared of nothing, and really, as I look back at the story, I realize the fish and the bucket of cold water meant pretty much nothing to me. I hardly even remember anything but the kid, just that kid who's out there on his own, the kid who's not scared.

Whatever the cost, that must be a great feeling to have. I wonder.

Jack Zipes

There is something putatively magical about an afterword. The term suggests that there is more worth saying than what has already been written, as if the afterword can provide a magic touch with a happy ending to a book that needs resolution.

But this book does not need closure or resolution. There is such a great variety and diversity in all the ruminations that they tend to open up the question about how men respond to fairy tales and keep the question open. It is almost impossible to spot or trace a "male aesthetic" or perspective in the attitudes toward the fairy tale. Whereas it is somewhat easy to detect a feminist approach to a fairy tale, whether written by a woman or a man, I find it difficult—at least, in this anthology—to sense a "masculine approach" or a particular male way of thinking. Perhaps if male athletes, workers, pop singers, cabdrivers, executives, and so on were to offer their views on fairy tales, it would be possible to discover distinctly male attitudes. But I am not certain, because most children, boys and girls, are enchanted and nurtured by the fairy tale, and the fairy tale has not been partial to one sex or the other.

Men have always loved fairy tales—loved to tell them, loved to hear them, loved to write them. Although the fairy tale has been more or less labeled a female, if not effeminate and infantile, affair and been disparaged since the late Renaissance as "feminine"—associated with Mother Goose, gossips, witches, grannies, and foolish ladies—more than anything else, this disparagement had to do with the Christian church's endeavor to brand secular and pagan tales as heretical and its campaign to proselytize and establish its authority through its own fantastic myths. The denigrating attitude was also connected to the development of canons of proper literature and the separation of high and low culture. Whatever was associated with women was generally excluded from high culture. Yet the fairy tale was never "feminine," never the property of women alone, though it might have been gendered in the way it was told and written. Men always told and wrote fairy tales. If we simply cast a glance at the prominent writers of literary fairy tales that have established the literary genre, they include mainly men, from Straparola and Basile through Perrault, the Brothers Grimm, Hoffmann, and Andersen to Hesse, Tolkien, Ende, and Coover. The classical genre has been framed by male authors, although it has certainly been challenged and subverted by women writers from the very outset in France and certainly during the last thirty-five years. And, men have also joined in the subversion.

This is the point well taken by Coover when he writes, "Tale is the underbelly of myth. Myth is head, tale body; myth power, tale resistance; myth nice, tale naughty," and so on. Coover's distinctions between myth and fairy tale are well worth noting, so long as we keep in mind that many fairy tales can also be somewhat conservative and have become mythicized, sanitized, and commercialized. But what hasn't been made into a commodity in the last fifty years? Walt Disney began the process as early as 1937 with his production of *Snow White and the Seven Dwarfs*, and since then his corporation has not stopped packaging the fairy tale like a sweet, to be consumed almost like a drug to avoid thinking about reality. Fortunately, even within the realm of the so-called culture industry there are printed and cinematic fairy tales such as *Shrek* that, while seeking to make money from viewers, offer resistance to the tamed fairy tale and are as naughty as can be.

But the best fairy tales are more than just subversive. They must be profoundly utopian even when they are dystopian. They must somehow touch our souls and innermost needs. After reading the essays, comments, poems, stories, and meditations in Kate Bernheimer's anthology, I have come away with the feeling that, when the fairy tale "works," it works itself into our bloodstream and never leaves. All the writers and artists who have contributed to this unusual book respond as though the fairy tale were part of their lives and continues to play a dynamic role in their creativity.

Recently I have been intrigued by the British biologist Richard Dawkins's theory of memes. He claims that, aside from the genes that determine the way we behave and think, there are also replicators that he calls memes, units of cultural transmission such as tunes, ideas, catchphrases, clothes fashions, and ways of making pots or of building arches. "Just as genes propagate themselves in the gene pool by leaping from body to body via sperms or eggs," he states, "so memes propagate themselves in the meme pool by leaping from brain to brain via a process which, in the broad sense can be called imitation." His theory may seem far-fetched to many, but Dawkins has put his finger on a feature of fairy tales that makes them so very relevant and memorable: they latch onto us, and we latch onto them; we absorb them, store them, and retell them because they concern our basic instincts and provide hope that we can adapt to a world that is absurd and out of our control. We spread and retell tales in our own way based on our own experiences so that no tale, no matter how classical it is, is ever told in the exact same way. The fairy tale, its very core, wants us to play with its characters, motifs, characters, and themes to find our own way through the dense woods. It cannot thrive without innovation, just as we cannot thrive without innovation.

This is the touchstone of Kate Bernheimer's anthology. Not knowing what to expect, she invited male writers and artists to offer their views on fairy tales, and her prodding has generated the unexpected. Indeed, I suspect her invitation was a kind of challenge to the men whom she addressed, and it reminds me of the tale about the merchant who was confident that nobody could tell a tale without beginning with "once upon a time" and ending with "and they lived happily ever after." This merchant was so sure of himself that he bet his store against any other property that no one could tell a fairy tale without the proper beginning and ending. Two brothers tried and lost their property to the merchant. Of course, there was a third brother, the youngest, who came and started his story, sure enough, with "once upon a time," but when he reached the end, he cried out, "You may be happy and content, but my brothers can no longer pay their rent!" And he took over the store and continued to tell tales that upset the expectations of his listeners and, at the same time, gave them food for thought.

Steve Almond is the author of *Candyfreak,* a memoir, and the short story collections *My Life in Heavy Metal* and *The Evil B. B. Chow and Other Stories.*

Brian Baldi recently received his MFA from the University of Massachusetts and has published in *Zyzzyva, Fairy Tale Review,* and elsewhere.

Christopher Barzak has published stories in a variety of literary and speculative fiction venues, including *Nerve, Realms of Fantasy, Lady Churchill's Rosebud Wristlet, Strange Horizons, Vestal Review, The Year's Best Fantasy & Horror,* and *Trampoline.*

Joshua Beckman is editor of *Wave Poetry* in Seattle. His books of poetry include *Nice Hat. Thanks,* with Matthew Rohrer; *Something I Expected to Be Different;* and *Things Are Happening,* which was selected by the poet Gerald Stern to receive the first *American Poetry Review* / Honickman First Book Award.

Greg Bills is the author of the novels *Consider This Home* and *Fearful Symmetry,* and he directs the creative writing program at the University of Redlands in California.

Jirí Cêch has appeared as a primary or peripheral character in many short stories and articles, including "Czechoslovakian Rhapsody Sung to the Accompaniment of Piano" and "Glauke's Gown," published in the *Iowa Review;* "Oops. Sorry," published in *Notre*

Dame Review; and "In Case You Haven't Noticed I'm Not Wearing Any Clothes," presented at Notre Dame's &NOW Festival of Writing as a Conceptual Art. His first book of poetry, *Whither: Poems of Exile,* won the Mennstrausse Poetry Award.

Alexander Chee is the author of the novel *Edinburgh.* That novel won the Lambda Editor's Choice Prize, and Chee has also been awarded a fellowship from the National Endowment for the Arts, and the Whiting Writers' Award. He lives in Rochester, New York, and has completed a new novel, the forthcoming *The Queen of the Night.*

Robert Coover is the author of many books, including, most recently, *A Child Again.* His first novel, *The Origin of the Brunists,* won the 1966 William Faulkner Award. His other works include the collection of short fiction *Pricksongs and Descants;* a collection of plays, *A Theological Position;* and such novels as *The Public Burning, Spanking the Maid, Gerald's Party, Pinocchio in Venice, John's Wife, Ghost Town,* and *Briar Rose.* His latest honor is the Dungannon Foundation's Rea Award for his lifetime contribution to the short story. He teaches in the Program for Literary Arts at Brown University.

Neil Gaiman writes books for readers of all ages and has long been one of the top writers in modern comics. His *New York Times* bestselling novel for adults, *American Gods,* was awarded the Hugo, Nebula, Bram Stoker, SFX, and Locus awards. His most recent collection, *Fragile Things: Short Fictions and Wonders,* debuted on the *New York Times* bestseller list.

Johannes Göransson was born and raised in Sweden but has lived in the United States since he was thirteen. He is a PhD candidate at the University of Georgia and teaches at Notre Dame. With his wife, Joyelle McSweeney, he coedits the press Action Books and the online quarterly *Action, Yes.* In the fall of 2005 Action Books published *Remainland: Selected Poems of Aase Berg,* which he translated.

Ilya Kaminsky was born in Odessa, in the former Soviet Union, in 1977, and he arrived in the United States in 1993, when his family was granted asylum by the U.S. government. He is the author of *Dancing in Odessa*, which won the Whiting Writers' Award, the Metcalf Award from the American Academy of Arts and Letters, the Dorset Prize, and the Ruth Lilly Fellowship, given annually by *Poetry* magazine. In addition, he writes poetry in Russian. His work in that language was chosen for "Bunker Poetico" at Venice Bienial Festival in Italy. In the late 1990s he cofounded Poets for Peace.

Eric Kraft is the author of the continuing novel *The Personal History, Adventures, Experiences & Observations of Peter Leroy*, which includes, so far, nine volumes: *Little Follies, Herb n' Lorna, Reservations Recommended, Where Do You Stop?, What a Piece of Work I Am, At Home with the Glynns, Leaving Small's Hotel, Inflating a Dog*, and *Passionate Spectator*. Kraft grew up in Babylon, New York, on the Great South Bay of Long Island. He is a graduate of Harvard College, holds a master's from Harvard University, and has taught school and written textbooks and was, for a time, part owner and cocaptain of a clam boat, which sank. He has been the recipient of a fellowship from the National Endowment for the Arts and the John Dos Passos Prize for Literature.

Norman Lock is the author of *A History of the Imagination, Notes to "The Book of Supplemental Diagrams" for Marco Knauff's Universe, Land of the Snow Men, Joseph Cornell's Operas/Émigrés, Trio, Plays, The Long Rowing unto Morning*, and *Cirque du Calder*. His stage plays include *Water Music, Favorite Sports of the Martyrs, Mounting Panic, The Sinking Houses, The Contract*, and *The House of Correction*—voted one of the best plays of 1988 and 1994 (for a revival) by the *Los Angeles Times* and critically acclaimed as the "best new play" of the 1996 Edinburgh Theatre Festival.

Gregory Maguire is the author of *Son of a Witch, Wicked, Confessions of an Ugly Stepsister*, and *Mirror Mirror*, among many other books.

Michael Martone's new book is *Michael Martone*, a memoir done in contributor's notes, many of which were originally published in the contributors' notes sections of various magazines. Some of his other books are *Seeing Eye, Pensées: The Thoughts of Dan Quayle, Fort*

Wayne Is Seventh on Hitler's List, Safety Patrol, and *Alive and Dead in Indiana. The Flatness and Other Landscapes,* a collection of his own essays about the Midwest, won the Association of Writing and Writing Programs (AWP) Prize for Creative Nonfiction in 1998. He teaches at the University of Alabama and lives in Tuscaloosa with the poet Theresa Pappas and their two children, Sam and Nick.

Michael Mejia is the author of the novel *Forgetfulness* and an assistant professor in the English department at Berry College in Berry, Georgia, where he teaches creative writing. He recently received a Fellowship in Literature from the National Endowment for the Arts.

Timothy Schaffert grew up on a farm in Hamilton County, Nebraska. His first novel, *The Phantom Limbs of the Rollow Sisters,* won the Nebraska Book Award for Fiction in 2003. His most recent novel is *The Singing and Dancing Daughters of God.* His short stories have appeared in *Prairie Schooner, Greensboro Review, Press, Natural Bridge,* and other literary journals, and he has received the Henfield/Transatlantic Review Award, the Mary Roberts Rinehart Award, and two awards from the Nebraska Arts Council. He now directs Omaha Lit Fest.

David J. Schwartz's fiction has appeared in such venues as *Lady Churchill's Rosebud Wristlet, Strange Horizons, The Third Alternative,* and the upcoming anthologies *Twenty Epics* and *Spicy Slipstream Stories.* His stories have been shortlisted for the Fountain Award and received honorable mention in *The Year's Best Fantasy and Horror.* He appears online at http://snurri.blogspot.com.

Vijay Seshadri is the author of two books of poems, *Wild Kingdom* and *The Long Meadow.* He teaches at Sarah Lawrence College and lives in Brooklyn with his wife and son.

Richard Siken, a New York City–born poet who now lives in Tucson, Arizona, is the author of *Crush. Crush* was the winner of the Yale Series of Younger Poets competition, the oldest annual poetry prize in the United States, and was a finalist for the 2005 National Book Critics Circle Award.

Kieran Suckling is policy director of the Center for Biological Diversity. He lives with his wife and daughter in Tucson, Arizona.

Maria Tatar is professor of German literature at Harvard University. She is author of *The Hard Facts of the Grimms' Fairy Tales, Spellbound,* and *Secrets beyond the Door: The Story of Bluebeard and His Wives.*

Jeff VanderMeer is a two-time World Fantasy Award winner whose books of fiction and edited anthologies have been finalists for the Philip K. Dick Award and the International Horror Guild Award. Books by VanderMeer have made the year's best lists of *Publishers Weekly,* Amazon.com, *LA Weekly, San Francisco Chronicle, Locus Magazine, Publisher's News,* and many more. He is best known for writing *City of Saints & Madmen* and *Veniss Underground,* and for coediting the *Leviathan* anthologies and *The Thackery T. Lambshead Pocket Guide to Eccentric and Discredited Diseases.*

Willy Vlautin was born and raised in Reno, Nevada. His first novel, *The Motel Life,* was published in Great Britain in 2006 and in the United States and France in spring 2007. He is a member of the internationally acclaimed band Richmond Fontaine and lives in Portland, Oregon.

Jack Zipes is professor of German at the University of Minnesota. An acclaimed translator and scholar of children's literature and culture, his most recent books include *Hans Christian Andersen: The Misunderstood Storyteller* and *Beautiful Angiola: The Lost Sicilian Folk and Fairy Tales of Laura Gozenbach.*

ABOUT THE EDITOR

Kate Bernheimer is assistant professor of English in the MFA Program in Creative Writing at the University of Alabama. She is the author of two novels, *The Complete Tales of Ketzia Gold* and *The Complete Tales of Merry Gold,* which are part of a roman fleuve, and editor of *Mirror, Mirror on the Wall: Women Writers Explore Their Favorite Fairy Tales.* Her first children's book, *The Girl in the Castle inside the Museum,* is forthcoming in 2008, and she edits the literary journal *Fairy Tale Review.*